Contents

2 The incubator

I was born on 20th April 1974 in Margate, the first born son of Margery and Richard, known as Dick, Stevens from Sandwich in Kent. I clearly do not remember my actual birth as no one does, and while I was clearly there, I do not see the events surrounding my birth as being directly connected to my lived experience.

I will discuss my family and home life in another chapter as I want to focus on the events surrounding my birth, and the few days or weeks after this. My understanding of what happened in imprecise as it is from the little nuggets of information I picked up from my parents and others during my childhood. It was never a subject I talked about with my parents, and for reasons that will become clear, something I have been unable to discuss with them as an adult.

My birth was a difficult one. Firstly, my mother was in labour for four days before I finally popped out, and this was only after there was no choice and she needed a cesarean. That was only the start of the problems that were going to have lifelong consequences for myself, and the people around me, and what makes the story my unique story.

While my mother was pushing me from the womb into the real world, my understanding is that my umbilical cord became wrapped around my neck tightly. So, while I was still inside my mother's tummy, I was being strangled, causing my brain, specifically the cerebellum, to be starved of oxygen. This meant my brain was now damaged, never to be repaired, which is called cerebral palsy, Latin for the paralysis of the cerebellum. I also heard from my mother that the situation had been made harder because one of the doctors was unavailable when the labour was becoming difficult, running late and playing golf! I do not really know what went on.

Cerebral palsy (cp), also known as Little's disease, affects 1% of the population worldwide. Its' effects are hugely varied and no one person with cp is affected precisely in the same way as anyone else. Broadly speaking, cp affected myself in terms of my walking, balance, speech and hand control.

At the stage, there is two important points to pick up on. The first is that it is important to understand that before my birth, the nine months I was growing in my mother's womb, I was a perfectly healthy child for all intents and purposes. It was the couple of minutes where I was being starved of oxygen that was going to have the greatest effect on my life than any other 'couple of minutes' since. I have sometimes wondered that if there was a parallel universe where I did not have cerebral palsy, how different would my life be. I never assumed that life was be any better, and often concluded I could have been worse off without cp, but that's my nature and I simply find it difficult to imagine life without cerebral palsy.

The second point is that I do not have any negative emotions about my birth or having cerebral palsy, indeed now or anytime in my life. By this I mean I have never been upset by the fact I have cerebral palsy as I see no reason to be. What happened has happened and from my perspective, it has always been a part of me and I do not know what it is like not to have cp. I do not remember the time just after my birth and therefore I have no dramatic event to handle as a lifelong memory in the same way as if I have had my impairment in later life.

I have the feeling that my mother was very much on her own in the days after my birth, and what I know of my father, he was probably not pulling his weight in supporting her. I have always felt from what a child picks up from their parents that my birth was a very dramatic event for my mother, something I never blamed myself for, and it had probably affected her mental health in some way to come. Her situation would not have made better by the fact the doctors and other staff will have known my birth would had not gone to plan, but would probably not have told my mother anything. This would have meant my mother could have felt isolated and vulnerable.

As I understand it, as soon as I was born I was put in an incubator, although I am not sure whether I was in one for a few days or weeks.

Since I have no conscious memories of being in an incubator and no photos were taken as far as I am aware, I can only imagine what the incubator looked like from what I have seen on television. So, I imagine a clear plastic 'box' with arm holes, which I would be lying in within an intensive care situation. For the days or weeks I lied there, this was be the totality of my sensory input.

Saying I have no conscious memory of the experience leads to the possibility of unconscious memories that could have had a fundamental effect on my personhood and how I would interact with society. This leads me to ask many questions about the impact being in an incubator may have had on who I am.

Being physically isolated from others and probably lacking the tactile touch most babies experience makes me wonder if was this the point I gained my independent nature and determination that this story will make apparent? Or did these qualities come before this point? Did the fact I did not spend quality time with my parents so early on in my life result in a strain in our relationship that could never really be repaired? Is this where I learnt that in the limited understanding of a baby, that if no-one is helping you, you must help yourself? That need to never fully trust others have your best interests in mind?

Being in the incubator, the doctors feared for my life as I was a fragile child to them, and so I was quickly baptised, presumably so I would end up in the right place in my afterlife. I guess my mother was rushed with little outside support to come up with a name for myself, and she choseme, and so a core part of my identity wascreated.

I have always been bemused by how and why my mother chose my name because it appears to have no links to my family's history. My bemusement comes from the fact my brother, Richard Frank John (Stevens), who was yet to exist until another 3 years and 20 days, was named after his father, grandfather and uncle. I have wondered if the pressure of the moment, my mother consciously or unconsciously named me after someone significant to her that few people may have been aware of like an ex-boyfriend. The different ways my brother's and mine names were chosen seemed to be symbolic to our different life paths. He had a very normal one in so many ways, which I will discuss further in the story, while I had a very strange one.

Once the doctors have concluded a very premature death was not on the cards, they told my mother the worst case scenario in terms of my life. I was never going to walk, or talk, or be able to do anything meaningful with my life. This little chat is not unusual as many parents of children with cp have reported a similar experience over many years. History and this story will demonstrate the doctors got it wrong on many levels.

Evidently at some point I became well enough to go home with my mother and so began my life now my course has been set.

3 The Early year

While I was born in Margate in Kent, and my parents were from Sandwich in Kent, I have no memory of living in Kent. My father was a police officer and so we moved to Horsham in West Sussex because of his work, and maybe so the immediate family could have a fresh start. As far as I was concerned, I lived throughout my childhood in the district of Horsham.

The first few years of my life, before I was 3 and I had any clear memories, are unclear to me. Like my birth, the understanding of events of my first 3 years are based on what I have picked up over the years from my parents and others. I am also unsure what order some events occurred in.

The first event I know very little about is when my mother was told that I had cerebral palsy. My mother and I left hospital with her knowing very little about my diagnosis although her observations was that there was clearly something wrong with me, but no one had told her it was cerebral palsy.

Apparently at some health visitor style appointment with a doctor, the doctor simply said sharply to my mother "oh, didn't you know your son was a spastic?!'. The term spastic was an acceptable term in 1974 to describe someone with cp, although it is now accepted as a derogatory term which no sane professional would now dare to use. My core identity label had been confirmed, the one that would have a great impact on my life ahead.

Either when I was one or two, I attended Ingfield Manner in Five Oaks near Horsham, a school run by the Spastics Society, now called Scope. The school was an especially for people with cp. My placement was short because apparently, I was not impaired enough to benefit from what the school offered at that time.

When I was 2, I assume upon reflection, I went to the infant unit of Roffey Hospital in Horsham, a mental hospital in the traditional sense, as a day patient/pupil. While I did not have learning difficulties, the professionals had not so far realised this and hence this was why I was placed here within a very different era of opportunities.

This is when I started to have memories, some of which are as crystal clear today as they ever were. One of my first memories was being fed lunch in the dining room of the hospital, or so I am always assumed. I also have a vague memory of painting wearing a plastic smock.

These are very dark days in terms of how people with significant impairments were treated by society, a million miles from the improvements we have now. Special schools were the norm, as well as residential care for adults. My opportunity as an impaired child or adult appeared very limited, Therefore the hospital and the fact I had been mislabelled was not something unusual, the fact, as the story will show, I broke free from this label is something almost unique.

During the mid1970s. the political climate locally in special needs education was changing and as a result the whole of the child 'learning difficulties' unit of the hospital, ages 3 to 19, was going to move into its own newly purpose built school. This was 1977/8 and the Queen was celebrating her silver jubilee. So, after same political negotiation from the school's new headmaster, Wyn Davies, it was arranged for the Queen to open the school as a part of her celebrations and hence the school was named 'Queen Elizabeth Silver Jubilee School for the Mentally Handicapped', or the QE2 as it would be known locally.

I was at the school on the day it was open and I have a vague memory of meeting the Queen although it seems distorted as I saw the Queen sitting on a throne. I also remember being unwell that day and not being allowed the jelly and cream being provided to guests and pupils.

Even before the school formally opened, when staff and pupils were settling in, including myself, the teachers had started to understand that maybe I did not have learning difficulties, and actually I was quite smart. On my office wall currently is a full page article about the opening of the school where I appear in all 3 of the photographs shown, including one specially focused on myself. I think the photographs show that even at such a young age that my intelligence and determination shined through naturally regardless of what labels were placed upon me.

I am not sure how long I was at the school, maybe 2 or 3 years, but it was a good time for me. My personality was already shining, and I was getting the opportunity to try many things like camping and a few days school trip to Jersey. I had also built up a good relationship with the 'kitchen ladies' including the head of the kitchen, Pat. While she first met me when I was 2, we remain friends right into my 20s and I believe it shows I had a desire for adult company from a young age, which is a theme I will return to.

Once the school had been established I did not have learning difficulties from their observations, it was decided that I should go a mainstream primary school. I am unsure how or why this decision was made as it would have been simpler to place me in a school for children with physical impairments. Looking back, in this era of the late 1970s, this was a very revolutionary idea as inclusion for someone with my level of impairment, particularly in terms of my speech, was unheard of.

Over a period of a few months I spent one morning a week at a number of schools for a few weeks at a time to see which one would be the most suitable. The conclusion to everyone's satisfaction was my local village school. My family and myself were now living in Slinfold, a few miles outside Horsham, where my father was the 'local bobby'.

So, at some point in the 1970s, I became a full time pupil of Slinfold Primary School. I don't really have a lot of memories from this period, not important ones anyway. I appeared for the most part to be fitting in. While I could walk, I was unsteady on my feet, so I used walking sticks in the playground. "Hit me with your rhythm stick" by Ian Jury was Number One, and so this is what my friends asked me to do at playtime, probably to the annoyance and frustration of the teachers.

I am not sure how it came about but a college student call Jill decided to do a video about myself as a piece of coursework, in an era where videoing was a new technology which was not as everyday as it is now. This caused a lot of excitement for the teachers and other pupils. I do not remember the contents of the video but I wish I had the opportunity to see it as an adult. Like with Pat from the QE2, I built up a long-term relationship with Jill that has lasted throughout my life.

I assume from my perspective that my placement at the school was going okay, but it seemed others had a different idea. The catchment area of the consisted of a lot of wealthy families and in the way a child picks up on vibes, I sensed there was probably 'concern' about my presence at the school, particularly in terms of my drooling.

Anyway, from reasons I am still not fully aware off, the placement failed and so I was transferred to another school as described in the next chapter. This could have been because the school did not feel able to continue to meet my needs, or because my confidence and determination shown in my speech and gross body movements, which were obvious when I was frustrated, was perceived as challenging, I really have no idea.

This chapter has reminded myself that even at such an early age, the combination of my impairment and my vocal determination were causing headaches for adults. It was most likely causing rules to be bent or even re-invented to handle my situation. This was all happening with me blissfully unaware of the trouble I was causing as I just got on with being myself. If this was my life before I was even 6, you can start to imagine the trouble I would be causing as I grew up.

The chapter also reminds me that without having contact to my family as I write this story, there are many gaps in my understanding to why specific events happened, and how these events were related to myself and how I developed. I did not move schools because my parents moved but because I challenged the system in a way that was just natural to me. It would however be nice to know more about the politics I was causing around me.

4 The PH years

In 1980, my parents separated for reasons I will explain in another chapter. Because we lived in a police house, it meant my mother, my brother Richard and myself had to move out. We ended up living in the middle of a garage and petrol station outside Horsham, at a junction between two main roads. The 'bungalow' was damp and the bedroom my brother and I shared had mould. This would be the catalyst that will either cause me to have lifelong asthma or at least bring it to everybody's attention.

It was not long before my mother found and fell in love with Brian, who in January 1982 became my step-dad. When I say fell in love, I am unsure if it was a true romance or a marriage of convenience. In September 1981, we all moved to 14 Depot Road in Horsham, which would remain my home throughout the rest of my childhood until I went to university in 1992.

In January 1981, I started school at Southgate First/Middle School's 'physically handicapped (PH) unit' in Crawley. This was a unit of two interconnecting classrooms that was attached to a mainstream school for children aged between 5 and 12. We shared the playground and other facilities with the main schools like the swimming pool.

Since I had to travel 8 miles each day to school, I was firstly picked up by a special school bus when I started at the school, and then by taxi when I moved to Depot Road. A number of children were picked up by the same taxi from Horsham and Crawley, and this would be my daily routine for a couple of years.

Like the QE2, I think it became obvious that I was very intelligent. While all the pupils had physical impairments, some had social skill issues. While we came together as a unit for some lessons, especially in terms of sports and arts, we very much worked academically on an individual basis and so it was hard to judge where other pupils were in their development. However, it did feel that I was doing a level of work more advanced than the other pupils were.

I remember that a lot of my academic work came from American text books, which is actually a different language with terms like sidewalk and railroad. My teacher, Mrs Jarvis, used to write down the Countdown Maths puzzles of the evening before for me to solve. While I was taking typing lessons, I was still writing full time with pen and paper, which was often illegible and full of drool marks.

The unit had a computer, a Commodore PET 4016 with just 16k of memory. It is important to understand computers were very different back then and they were only mainly used by big businesses. I however took to the computer like a duck to water and I was making it do things that others could not, easily surpassing the knowledge of the teachers. I also do not remember any other pupil using the computer. As a result of using a computer at school, my parents brought me one to use at home.

The computer in all its many reincarnations would remain a vital tool to my ability to express myself on my own terms to ever increasing levels of influence. The head of computing within the main school took some pupils to an International Commodore show in London, which included myself and my parents, where we had a stand showing off using computers within schools. Many professionals at the show were totally amazed at the fact I was using a computer and the potential that this meant for the future.

Maths had always been my favourite and best subject. As a result, I attended Maths lessons in the main school with the non-impaired pupils as well as other lessons. One of the purposes of the unit was to 'integrate' pupils into the main school wherever possible. I am not sure many other pupils in the unit had this opportunity but I made the most of this as this grew through my four years at the school. One week, I believe off my own back, I attended mainstream lessons for the whole day to see how well I could cope, which did not seem to last very long but I enjoyed it.

I was clearly headed in the right direction in terms of being independent and able to function in a mainstream environment. I remember Mrs Jarvis, my teacher and the head of the unit, telling me that I would have to work twice as hard to compete with my non-impaired peers. I have always taken this to heart and worked 3 or more times harder than anyone else to achieve what I wanted in life, always naturally going that extra mile.

I was also starting to develop my defence mechanisms at my time at the school. I remember for a few weeks this other pupil from the unit, who appeared to be physically unimpaired, was taunting me, pushing me and running away. He was clearly faster than me but one time, I caught him, dragged him to the ground and I had him in an arm lock until Mrs Jarvis came running out. She said afterwards in her office I could had killed him, which was not exactly true. I said I was glad and I still remain glad to this day because I instinctively fought back.

The afternoons in the unit were mostly the softer subjects like art, music and sport. My favourite of these were swimming and horse riding. For horse riding, we had to go to a riding school by minibus, and I remember at the time hating having the wear the yellow harnesses on the bus. As a result of going horse riding which was organised by 'Riding for the Disabled', I went on a number of riding holidays particularly for disabled children which were enormous fun.

My greatest achievement at the school was designing the certificates for the Inter-school sports day. Each year the various special schools in the area, including the QE2 and Southgate, would come together for an afternoon of competitive sports, which were events designed to match the abilities of participants. Each year a different school would host the event and during my last year at the school, we hosted the event.

Using the unit's computer, I designed the certificate, which were photographed onto green paper and stuck on brown cardboard. This may sound nothing special in this era of smartphones for the masses, but for the fact a 11 year old with cerebral palsy was doing desktop publishing 5 years before the term existed on a device with a billionth of the memory and power of the average smart phone is absolutely amazing. It is also somehow typical for myself in terms of pushing the boundaries of technology.

Outside school, I did not have many of my school friends visited me because of the distances involved in travelling due to the unit's large catchment area. I did however attend a mainstream Cub Scouts group. I found Cubs really complimented school and taught me all the things they don't teach at school like first aid and tying knots.

I was deeply proud when I became a sixer of my patrol, Greys. As the only cub with impairments within the pack, it showed that not only could I participaet within the Scouts movement, but I could also lead my non-impaired peers on for the most part on an equal footing. When there were activities with something that I would find difficult, I would find a way to 'bend the rules' fairly so I could take part, a tool that has always helped me. As a sixer, I was a good leader and I believe I was good in involving everyone which made us a successful patrol.

In 1985, aged 10/11, it was time to look at where my next school would be. Southgate had been a very comfortable time for me, like any primary school should be, but it was now time for big school. Because of my impairments, there was a number of options to where I could go, but there were just two options that stood out.

The first option was Lord Mayor Treloars in Hampshire. This was and remains a leading academically focused residential school for children with physical impairments. My parents and I spent the day looking it at the school. It was okay and it had a lot of facilities but seeing all the impaired pupils in their uniforms looking like robots, the thought that entered my head was I did not want to be normal by going to a special school.

The second option was my local all-boys mainstream secondary school, Forest Community School. This was the school my step-father went to in his time as a teenager, and the school would be where my brother would naturally attend. This would be a colossal thing for everyone involved as this was an era where people with my level of impairment did not attend mainstream schools. Some of the teachers from the school visited me at Southgate to see if it was going to be feasible and they thought it was.

I believe my parents appeared to have given me the choice of which school I would attend and I chose Forest Boys, as it was mostly known locally, because I felt I was up for the challenge of attending a 'normal school'. The question would be would the school itself be up for the challenge ahead.

5 Going to normal school

In September 1985, I started Forest Boys as a fully pledged full-time no going back pupil. I strongly believe you can not underestimate how pioneering my placement at the school was, a school of over a thousand non-impaired pupils. Imagine being a teacher with classes of 30 pupils being told you are going to have a pupil in your class that walks funny, does not talk properly and can not write or draw to any suitable standard, which you would need to manage unsupported? Imagine also being told that this was not an experiment that would last a few days or weeks to see if this was going to work, but rather like it or not, this was permanent!

My personal tutor was Mrs Battersby, who was also the head of the special needs department, which was mostly focused at that time on 'slow learners'. In the early years, she appeared to be interfering too much with my affairs but on reflection I think she was dealing with a lot of issues that were arising from my placement. Years after I had left the school I made contact with her and she told me how she needed to literally 'counsel' some of the teachers who were concerned about how to teach me.

Ironically, the person who seemed least prepared for my presence at the school was the headmaster, Dr Frank Newby. He was a traditional headmaster who retired in my final year at the school and I am convinced he agreed to my presence because he saw it as a gimmick that could be used to promote his school and himself. Because he was not a hands on sort of person, he left the chaos I was unintentionally causing to others to sort out.

For myself, I was taking my placement in my stride for the most part. A week before I started at the school I had a part of my left foot's big toenail removed, because it was in-growing. This meant that I started school wearing my mother's shoe on one foot, which I was worried the other pupils would think was a natural part of my impairment.

Right from the start, accepting there were many problems, I did not feel alienated even when I was. This was an era when I was easily be the only identifiable person with impairments for miles around, and this was something that was normal for me. As I will discuss later in the story, I was the freak and I had to develop mechanisms to accept, embrace and utilised this role.

I was at this school during my teens and at a time where like my peers, I was trying to establish who I was in terms of mmy self-identity. This was made difficult by the fact I was the only person with cp at the school and in my everyday interaction with others more generally. As a result, I believe I experienced something I have always called 'Ugly Duckling Syndrome'. As the title suggests, it is based on the idea that while I knew I was different I did not know really what that meant. As my peers were talking and walking normally, like looking in the mirror provided to me, I assumed on a day to day level, I was doing the same even though I knew that was not as fast or gracious. It was not until I was 17 until I started understanding what 'being disabled' meant. I believe my supposed naivety about the effects of my impairment kept my sane and able to compete with my peers as I did not worry about my difficulties.

Academically, the school was very good for me and I believe I received a proper and decent education. I am unsure if this would have been the case if I had gone to a special school, and so this had been one of my reasons of choosing Forest Boys. In most of my subjects, I was in the top set and I seemed to be able to match my peers with little trouble.

During my first weeks at the school I was writing with pen and paper with mixed success. I was quickly provided with my first laptop, an Epson HX20, which I had not realised until recently was the first laptop ever made. It had a keyboard, small screen and most importantly a built-in printer that printed out like supermarket receipts. So, I was printing out my work on till paper which was then cut into strips and glued into my exercise books ready for my teachers to mark. By my fourth year, the laptop was on its last legs and I managed to convinced the local education authority to purchase me a Cambridge

Z88, which was like the tablet of the day although far more primitive. In 1986, I upgraded my home computer from the Commodore PET to the BBC Master 128, providing me one of many quantum leaps in what I was able to achieve using technology.

I believe that one advantage of going a mainstream school compared to a special school was the fact it provides children with social skills that are often missed in special schools. Social skills are the manners and social norms that helps you interact with person in any setting from work to personal relationships. I have always been a good communicator despite my speech impairments, and while my social skills were not always spot on when I was younger, for the most part, it was on par with my non-impaired peers. If I upset people it is generally because I intended to do so. However, because of my speech impairment, drooling and jerky movements, my presence was not as polished as I would have liked it.

As well as the assistance in terms of technology, I also had a range of other assistance including a taxi still to and from school and help with carrying my bag between lessons from a member of admin staff. I did not do PE (and I believe this is why I missed out on sex education) and I used this time with an one-to-one helper to catch up on project work and other activities.

During science lessons, I had help from Linda Slattery, who happened to be the mother of my best friend, Mathew. She helped me with doing and writing up experiments and other activities. Over the five years I was at the school, the arrangement built up to the point she was not only helping me during my exams, writing for me on the exam paper as I would dictate, but also negotiating the special arrangements I could have with the exam boards. In many ways, she was my first personal assistant.

Finally, Forest Boys was just around your corner from the QE2 as well as sharing a large field with the school, and so I used to go there twice a week for physiotherapy and speech therapy. I used to go straight over the field as opposed to walking around. Since these sessions were just before lunch, I used to see Pat in the kitchens and stay for a bit of lunch, especially as Pat always had a nice treat from M&S for me like a small trifle. Over the years and long before I understood my mental health, these were important breaks from the stresses and strains attending a mainstream school.

The main disadvantage of going to a mainstream school was the fact I was bullied. I was taunted and bullied throughout my time at the school with very little respite. Each year the players and taunts would change but the consistency would remain the same. The message from Dr Newby was 'boys will be boys' and it seemed that bullying was not only accepted but also embraced in this era where child abuse in its broadest definition was not taken seriously.

While for many people, being bullied makes them withdrawn and feel isolated, it simply made be angry and frustrated. If it was allowed by Dr Newby and other teachers so I would learn my place in society, i.e the bottom of the pile, it was failing. Dr Newby basically told me to get used to it because I would be bullied all my life, which I discovered was never the case. The last time I was bullied was just a few years ago in a very different context.

I think one of the reasons I was bullied was a few weeks after I started at the school, all my peers where told to treat me normally when I was not in the room without any real explanation to what my difficulties meant. So, in the mind of 11 years old children, they did not see the difficulties I was facing but simply the extra things I appeared to be getting like a laptop and not doing PE, because it was never explained to them.

I do not blame the many pupils who bullied me nor have any malice towards them because there were merely a product of the system and culture of abuse for a better term created by Dr Newby and others. It was a product of its time and while I am sure that bullying has not been eradicated from schools, I am sure it is not the same culture of abuse or level of harshness.

For most of my time at Forest Boys my best friend was Matthew, who was and I believe still remains a geek, although I have not had any real contact with him since I left 6th form college. Our connection was based on computers and he helped me a lot with making them most of my laptops. Together we set up a very small commercial venture called SoftEx Software producing and selling our own computer magazine within the school, using my colour printer. Like doing the certificates at my previously school, this was still a very innovative use of what technology could achieve at the time. It was also the start of an active step towards what would become my lifelong dream of running my own company, which is at the heart of my journey.

The emotional distanced I seemed to have with my peers seem to be momentarily improved when we all went on the annual outward bounds week in the Lake district for the 4th years. I went with my step-dad to assist me with my care needs for the week. I did a range of activities equal to everyone else including canoeing and orienteering. One evening, some of teachers arranged some abseiling which I took part in. It was videoed and as some of the pupils watched it that evening afterwards, for a while there was a new-found respect for me.

In my 5th year, it was time to do my exams. This was when a lot of special arrangements were put in place, including the assistance from Linda. I always did my exams in a side room away from everyone else as I often had extra time, and so I could tell Linda what to write without disturbing everyone else. Apart from this, I was doing the exams on an equal basis to my peers.

I left Forest Boys in July 1990 with 9 GCSEs including A in Maths, and a RSA in Statistics. My placement at the school had been a challenge for everyone involved, but one I did not regret. During my time at the school, I had toughened up, maybe too much as I developed many defence mechanisms against being hurt emotionally by others. By my 3rd year, I was starting to have a voice and say what I needed as I realised no one else was going to do this for me, a lesson that remains important to me.

Fundamentally, I left the school stronger and ready to take my place in society as someone who was going to be fully included whatever anyone else thought. However, this achievement came at a price, and there was damage under my emotional bonnet I was yet to discover.

6 Family conflicts

I have waited until now to properly discuss my family because I wanted to put it in a proper context in terms of the other events in my childhood. It can be generally said that my relationship with my immediate family, especially during my adulthood, has not been great and basically non-existent. I am going to discuss each member of my immediate family in turn before explaining some of the issues related to them. I am not going to discuss my extended family as I have never had any real relationship with them, certainly not in my own right.

Let us start with my mother, Margery. Like I assume all mothers, she has played a central role in my development good or bad whether I liked it or not. I do not know too much about her background although I know it was one of absolute poverty and hardship where she played the Cinderella role to her brothers and mother as her father died when she was young.

My mother certainly had anger management issues, which I have inherited to a point, and it was always unpredictable to what mood she was in. She would be able to turn bringing her a cup of tea in the morning a few minutes too early or late into a day-long shouting match with such venom that it was unreal. She blamed it on her PMT, then her thyroid but from what I now know about myself, I believe she must had some undiagnosed mental illness issues that fundamentally affected her interaction with others. I am not sure if she was able to express love and it was she certainly found it a conscious effect to show affection.

Her mood swings dominated my relationship with her. If I could make it through a day I had to spend with her without her raising her voice then it was a good day indeed. I frequently have a reoccurring dream about her where a nice day is quickly turned sour by her rage. As someone so sensitive to other people's emotions for various reasons, her rage used to consume me wanting me to escape myself. Therefore, I used to ensure I spent as little time in her presence as possible as soon as I was old enough to do so with my limitations.

I am not sure if she loved me or if indeed I loved her, or even if we were capable of loving each other. We could both play the game of happy families but it was and felt meaningless. I therefore set my sights on bigger things, knowing I did not have her support since I did not have her understanding. I am not sure she ever really knew who I was.

My real father, as opposed to my step father, was someone I did not know very well. He left my life full time when I was 6 or 7, and then it was just spending a typical divorcee day with him once a month where he would treat myself and my brother to a nice day out. He would go on to marry 4 or 5 times in total, including a 18 year old when he was in his 40s, having two further children who I have had little contact with.

If there was one word to describe him, it would be selfish, which seemed to work very well for him as I envy to a point his ability to be selfish. I am not sure what else to say about him. He did not put much effort into trying to have any relationship with myself and therefore I am unsure if he deserves any credit for how I am now shaped. The only thing he has given me is a problem with alcohol which is something I will discuss later in the story.

My brother, Richard, is exactly 3 years and 20 days younger than me, and exactly opposite to me in so many ways. The fact he did not have significant impairments has meant we had very different experiences as children and adults despite the fact we both went to Forest Boys. We did play many games together as younger children but we grew apart as we got older.

Our relationship was not helped by the fact our mother would appoint him to the role of older brother, which annoyed us both. Some people could argue he was what people would now call a young carer but I am not sure he was as he was just assisting me as opposed to looking after me. He helped me, often reluctantly, with shirt buttons, shoes and so on. But he did not have to think for me and I would help in terms of thinking as we thought through problems together.

Richard used to bully and tease me a lot throughout my childhood which our mother seemed to encourage. I think this is because I was quite a loud character while he was the quite a silent type as far as I saw, and this was maybe his way of seeking attention. As we grew older, it was clear that he was becoming embarrassed of me. This was not so much because I had cerebral palsy, but because in his words, I acted disabled, being proud of how I was as opposed to hiding it as I presume he wished I did.

My step-father, Brian, came into my life when I was 7 and very much took on the role of being my 'dad' in the social sense. On one level, we got on well but there was a sinister side to our relationship. He was in no way slow but he was weak in terms of having his own uninfluenced opinions. Probably coming from a middle-class family that has messed up his views with contradictory guidance, he was an easy target for the dominating figure of my mother, who could make him perform like a dancing seal if she so wished.

He basically took his frustrations over being controlled by my mother upon myself, someone he saw sometimes foolishly as an easy target. This was not something I just observed but something he consciously told me on a few occasions. His frustrations resulted in violence towards me where he would too often wallop me or pin me on the wall by my throat, even when I was in my 20s. However, there was one time, on holiday in Portugal when I was an adult I walloped him back sending his spectacles flying. That was the last time he ever touched me because he now knew I would probably harm him if he tried it again. I was also now determined never to tolerate violence towards myself.

I have many half and step brothers and sisters, too many to count with probably a few I have not ever been told about, and certainly many I have not met. None of them have played a part in my life and therefore they are not people I can talk about here.

In talking about my immediate family as a whole, there are a few things which can be said. The first thing is that I feel I did not fit in.

Again, this was not because I had cerebral palsy, but because my life experiences and opportunities as a child and an adult were on a different level to them. Everyone else in my immediate family fitted into what could be seem as average, while I never did anything which was average. This is not to say I was any better than them, but I just lived in a different world to them which this story will explain. It has felt similarly to when someone from a working-class background ends up in a middle class career but does not seem to now fit into either class. My social class has also been something I have personally been unclear about as social media gave me opportunities beyond class.

I should be a son or brother anyone would be immensely proud off, which those who have read my whole story will learn. But for some reason, my family seem not to be impressed, or show they were impressed, and often simply saw my impairments and the practical difficulties I have and had as a child.

The second point is while it has been difficult to admit and acknowledge to myself until recently, I was abused physically and emotionally as a child by my mother, my step-father and my brother by varying degrees. As a child, it was never something to write home about but it existed and I have many vivid memories of being physically attacked for what I can only see as unnecessary reasons if there were any justification. Some people may say this is why I am now often asking policy makers to be weary of parents and carers, because of my bitter experiences. In fact, the truth is far from this, my concern is when children with impairments do not have a voice, and I felt I did as I could fight back.

This abuse made the need to escape them more necessary, even if it was unconscious at the time. Their actions have made me very much against any deliberate use of violence or shouting in this way, particularly when the parent is not quite in control of what they are doing and it is used as a method to express frustration or anger imposed upon someone else. When I see a parent shouting carelessly in the street to their upset child, not helping the situation at all, I have to stop myself saying something as I start to growl.

Overall, I feel there is a secret my immediate family has which I was not been let into me that is about me in some way and has fundamentally damaged our now non-existent relationship in a way I can not understand. I was never significantly naughty or aware of doing something so hurtful it would warrant this behaviour. My impairments made me rough around the edges and I was naturally loud but that all I can think off. It may be just in my head although I know there is something I am unaware off which has appeared to have caused significant damage.

I am unsure if my family were supportive outside the norms of behaving as a functional family to the outside world, or whether my emotional independence from them meant that they simply let me get on with what I wanted to do. I am also unsure if it was not me who did not let them in as I was determined to live my life in the way I intended to regardless of what anyone else thought, and maybe this was a defence mechanism from the abuse I received from them? Sadly, I am unlikely to ever find out.

7 College rebirth

After Forest Boys, the natural choice for me was doing my A-Levels at Collyer's 6th Form College in Horsham as that was where most of my peers were going. It was a mixed mainstream college with a lot of stairs. I decided to do A-Level Maths, Business Studies and Economics. I also decided to give up Economics after the first term as I needed more time for the other subjects.

Collyer's was a fresh start for me to begin to frame myself as a young adult away from the general hostility of Forest Boys. There was no bullying through my time at the college but rather new freedoms and opportunities for me to take advantage off in preparation to going to university. I really immersed myself into what the college could offer.

While the college was a much friendlier atmosphere for me, there was still unconscious barriers to making new friends in any deep and meaningful way. While I fitted in more than I did at Forest Boys, I was still very different to other students in many ways and still had a greater connection to adults older than myself.

In terms of meeting my impairment related needs, I was still having a taxi to and from college. I also had a Toshiba PC laptop for my Maths lessons. The business studies course required the use of computers by every student so I had an advantage over the other students. At home I had upgraded to an Acorn Archimedes, providing another quantum leap in what I was able to achieve from the comfort of my own bedroom.

The level and pace of the work required by both Maths and Business Studies were far more than it was at school, and it took me a while to adapt, especially with maths. A-Level Maths is very different when you are unable to draw by hand, and I had to adapt the technology around me. I had a great maths teacher, Mrs Broadhurst, who did not let me get away with anything. My business studies tutor was Mr Nicholls, who was also my personal tutor.

Since I was only doing two subjects I had plenty of unsupervised free time I could use for coursework etc. I used to spend most of the time in the computer room, which almost became my own private office when it was not being used for lessons.

He allowed me to use the college's modem to contact Bulletin Boards, which was the internet before the internet that gave me an insight to the opportunities of being online. He however slightly regretted it when he received a phone bill for £600! He wrote it off as an useful experiment.

Technology was really starting to liberate me and allow me to make a meaningful contribution to others. Desktop publishing had become mainstream and I was using it effectively. I was producing newsletters for two clubs I was involve in outside the college; Billingshurst PHAB and 'Ready and Able Club'. At the college, I entered and won 2 competitions to design a summer fete poster, as well as the 1992 Yearbook's cover.

One of the biggest achievements I had at the college was to have the drama department produce a full performance of a play I had written called Normality. Normality was about my experiences at Forest Boys based on a fictional day in a fictional setting. It was also about the paradox of feeling normal inside while at the same time rejecting the idea of having to be normal, which is a concept relevant today to me as it was in 1991.

The college adapted the play from an all-boys environment to a mixed environment. The main character, Frank, based on my own experiences, was clearly played by non-disabled actors. Interestingly, there were two people who played Frank on alternate nights, one of which was a girl, still playing Frank as a boy. As the play was short, it was billed with another play on mental health called 'FInd me'.

I attended each of the 4 performances as well as going to the wrap party. I did not socialise at all really with my peers outside college so this was an important step for me, and my opportunity to experience normality. It was also my opportunity to begin to bring my unique story to the world in the way I am doing now.

In the second year at college, it was time to do two things; find a university and do my exams. While I had considered for a time needing an extra year at the college and even not applying to University, i felt in the end that as most of my peers were applying to university, so should I. At that time I was applied, there were universities and polytechnics.

I realised that while I would pass my A-Levels, my grades were not going to be the best. Already my desires were moving away from simply academia being my savour into a broader range of opportunities. So, I looked at polytechnics and applied to Anglia, Bournemouth, and Coventry. I will discuss the outcome in another chapter.

The business studies course did not have any exams, relying solely on coursework. So, I only needed to focus on my Maths exams. Not being able to draw as well as needing to write complex formulas created a few challenges in terms of doing the exams. The solution was to do it in the computer room using two computers at the same time including my computer from home. With double time for each exam, making them 6 hours each, it was an exhausting time for me.

I left the college with a D in A-Level Business Studies and a B in A-Level Maths, which I was especially pleased about. The college was a good time for me and a time where I felt included in an innocent and safe environment. There was hard work, and challenges, but nothing felt impossible. It was also a stepping stone to my ultimate freedom that would be offered to me by going to University.

8 I am disabled

I have always known I had an impairment, cerebral palsy, but because I had it since birth, I did now know anything different and I had nothing to compare it with. My impairment was to me like having brown hair, brown eye and indeed five fingers; just one of those things in life I had no control about. It was only when I was 17 that I realised I was disabled, and what that meant for me, being a part of a socially oppressed minority.

In order to understand more about how I was feeling about the situation, it is important for me to explain briefly the models of disability in terms of the medical model and the social model. It is important to understand that at aged 17 that I did not have a formal understanding of these models but from my own observations, these models were already informally affecting my thinking.

The medical model has existed as a social construction since the start of the industrial revolution when the creation of factories meant the individual productivity to operate machinery was being measured, and those who could not do the amount expected from the average worker were deemed to be 'disabled'.

In this context, impairment and disability was pretty much the same thing, something to be seen as naturally biologically inferior. The model therefore states that my problem is my cerebral palsy, causing me to have abnormal speech and body movement that society finds uncomfortable. The solutions are simple; try to cure me or eradicate me.

The problem with this was I never saw my cerebral palsy as a problem and certainly not my problem even if others wanted to make it a problem for them. I understand that it has created challenges for but that this has been about how society and my environment has related to my impairment. And this lead me to understand and live the foundations of the social model long before I understood what it meant.

The social model was created by disabled people in the 1970s, and to be more specific, middle class white people with spinal injuries, a point that will have importance further in the story. It basically stated that it was not people's impairments that disabled them but rather their environment. Therefore, it could be argued that stairs disabled wheelchair users, as opposed to their inability to walk, and the solution is to build ramps and lifts.

On a social policy level, the social model has been fundamental in how society has improved within my lifetime for people with a range of impairments, even if some people with impairments currently do not have an appreciation for how much things have changed.

So, at 17, after a lifetime of not really having any real political interest in dysability issues, seeing my cerebral palsy as simply a part of my life, I was starting to understand I had a political identity as a disabled person. In 1991, disability was not framed in the mainstream as a political issue with no rights legislation on the books, having to wait until 1995 for that to happen with the Disability Discrimination Act.

Like any young person suddenly realising that the world was fundamental lyunfair, especially towards them, I was a bit of an arse about it for a year or so. This youthful expression towards perceived oppression is nothing new and protest in all its forms is a rite of passage for many people. I refuse to say now I am older, like people told me, that young people grow out of their idealisms, but we do learn that life is more complex and need smarter solutions. This is why I can understand the current appeal of Jeremy Corbyn even if I can't stand the man myself.

It was not until I had the opportunity to meet other disabled activists, I realised I did not really want to behave like them going forward. I was frustrated at the many ways I was discriminated on a frequent basis, but I did not appear to have the same of bitterness as other activists had, or distain for non-impaired people. I did not necessarily disagree with other activists' intentions, but I did feel there were better ways of achieving improvements. The difference so early on in my dysability career would have huge implications.

At 17, there were a number of dysability related issues that nagged me. The first was the use of the term Handicapped, which I really hated at a time it was still acceptable in some quarters. The term portrayed a level of vulnerability, specifically in terms of children, and it sounded very old fashion. Over time, I developed an understanding of the importance of language that went far beyond the failings of political correctness. Language and using it accurately would be very important to me as I understood how different but similar words had subtle but important different meanings.

As someone who mostly walked and had a speech impairment, one of my greatest frustration that still haunts me is being mistaken for someone who has learning difficulties. This was not because I have any menace towards anyone with learning difficulties but rather that my intelligence was my main tool to claim my inclusion into society whether I had the right or not. My appearance has meant that throughout my life I have always had long hard stares from young children, particularly on public transport, which I have often taken as one of those things I mostly find simply amusing.

I also remember being concerned that as someone who walked, I was often treated differently than people who use wheelchairs. On Saturday afternoons, I used to attend a PHAB (Physically Handicapped Able Bodied) youth club in Billingshurst for impaired and non-impaired young people. I remember playing Basketball as a group and feeling that my needs as someone with poor hand control was being ignored in comparison to the needs of those using wheelchairs. I think it made me committed to ensure the needs of everyone regardless of their impairments should be met.

The awakening of my impairment and disability identities was something that could only grow further over time. I would never fully understand why on a spiritual level why I had impairments and what that meant in the big scheme of life as someone who believed in his own form of destiny. Over the years, I would view the issues of dysability in every way possible to provide a rounder viewpoint of the subject.

Adulthood was upon me and I was a now a disabled person who planned, and was indeed destined to make a huge impact to the dysability agenda.

9 The end of youth

So, the story has reached 1992, when I am 18. Despite the predictions made about me just after my birth, I was doing pretty well for myself. Right from the beginning, it was clear I was destined to make a big difference to the world as I had always been making big waves by my determination to be fully included into society.

My actions to have a normal life, for a better term, seemed normal and without frustration. This is the way it was going to be because I did not expect anything else, and anyone, regardless of who they were, would have to simply get with it, choosing to do it the easy way or the hard way. This attitude still stays with me, softer or harder as it needs to be at different times.

At 18, normality was simply an unconscious part of what was required to be included in society. It was about conforming naturally, as far as I felt it was appropriate to do to how my non-impaired peers were behaving. It was never a problem or anything I became frustrated about. I was at an age where my youthful energy meant I had more flexibility to do things in a less effective way without realising it.

Now in my 40s, normality is certainly not a priority for myself and I believe my 18-year-old self may be surprised at who I am now. This story will show the transition between the important point in my life at 18 and now. I do find it interesting in how I have evolved and how the changing environment of society has enabled and empowered me to evolve gradually, becoming the person I am now happy to be.

Leaving college and going to University was an important step as this is when I became my own person who was truly responsible for their own actions, including my own finances. My parents played a diminishing role in my life in a way that I feel was quicker than a lot of people my age because this is what I wanted. My freedom as an adult would only come from a clear break from my parent's influences.

Without realising it at the time, my youthful and truthful independence and meaningful inclusion as someone with a significant impairment meant I was a part of an elite group who had made a significant step forward in overcoming the lack of autonomy that enabled the exclusion of others.

Around the world, too many people with significant impairments of all ages are directly or indirectly controlled by others, who hold ultimate responsibility for them and their lives, even if the individual themselves is fooled into believing the illusion they are somehow independent. But for me at 18 onwards, there was no one above me as the butt well and truly stopped with me!

This reality has always scared the pants off some people as they feel the need to be reassured that I was not in full control of my actions. When I am out on my own, I have often been asked who I was with where people were expected me to say that I was with my family or my carer. When I simply say 'me', they tend to go slightly white and start looking around me to see if this was indeed the case.

It was often exciting to know that considering my background, I was able to do want I wanted when I wanted how I wanted within the limits of my impairments and taking on the responsibilities associated with my actions. The trick was learning the boundaries of this new freedom, and over time I learnt how to push it to its limits.

Adulthood came with the realisation that at times my journey would be a lonely one. Too often I would be the only visibly impaired person in the room at meetings and conferences unless I attended a disability specific event although that was never always guaranteed. Even amongst other people with impairments I would most likely be the only one with a speech impairment unless I went to an event specifically for people with cerebral palsy. My work and inclusive attitude meant I spent most of my time with non-impaired people, which I found natural. Upon reflection, it has been interesting that I have often had better relationships with non-impaired people as opposed to those with impairments, certainly often in terms of my work.

Having cerebral palsy had meant firstly that I had to develop unique skills to enable me to use my impairment as a part of my strengths as opposed to my weaknesses. I often did this by using the power provided by being a 'freak'. For myself, the term freak is a positive and powerful term as it describes the realities of my appearance and its failure to conform to society's norms. Wearing a suit or presenting myself to be 'normal' would never work for me so I had to develop my own unique personality and social skills.

Being a freak meant people were not often expecting to see me in the context they had met me in. If there was a general book of social norms, they would now be looking fanatically for the page on how to deal with someone like myself, which they would not find. This firstly gives me time to take the upper hand as they became momentarily flabbergasted, and secondly, since there were no rules to how to interact with me in that situation, it enables me to write the rules myself on how the conversation is going to proceed. I have therefore turned a potential negative attribute into a positive one.

The other side of my loneliness was the fact that because I had a mainstream education with little contact with other people with impairments, it meant I did not always relate with other people with impairments at that time. This was not because I felt better than them but rather I had little to relate with them, especially those of the same age as myself who lacked social skills or the desire for intellectual conversation.

This was in fact true to a degree with my non-impaired peers as I preferred adult company and adult conversation in that respect. I believe this was because my experiences of mainstream education in terms of having to understand my own needs so I could communicate them to those who should have been assessing them on my behalf, meant I had to grow up quickly, and deal with adults in a manner my non-impaired peers did not have to. Therefore, I learnt to work and socialise with adults, as well as negotiating with them to achieve what I wanted.

So, I was no longer a child and adulthood awaited me unprepared for the wonderful mayhem I would be causing as I pushed the boundaries in ways no one could imagine.

10 University freedom

In choosing Anglia, Bournemouth and Coventry Polytechnics to apply to, it was Coventry who ended up having the privileged of accepting me. The first time I visited Coventry with my step-father was the Polytechnic's Open Day in early 1992. We parked by the Polytechnic and the first thing that struck me was how tall the buildings seemed to be.

The year I applied to the polytechnic, the government was making big changes to the higher education sector, turning all the polytechnics into 'new' universities. This meant that while I applied to Coventry Polytechnic, I ended up going to Coventry University, which was a nice bonus.

Coventry University was a city centre campus that was literally a few minute's walk from the city centre. It had at that time just one complex of student accommodation as the main 'Halls of Residence', where I would be stay for the first two years. Everything I needed for my time at the University for in easy walking distance, which was perfect for me.

As soon as I looked around the campus on the open day I felt this was the place for me and that this could be my home. There was nothing specific I could identify that led me to this thinking as it was more a general feeling. This was the biggest decision of my life so far with far reaching consequences for everything that would follow after this.

So, on 28th September 1992, I started my degree at Coventry University as I moved into my room in Priory Hall, the University's Hall of Residence, which was overlooking Coventry Cathedral. I had now made the first step of leaving home with £30 in my bank account and a fridge full of chocolate supplied by my parents.

It is important to understand that financially being a student in 1992 was very different to what it is now. There were no tuition fees to pay and at least until no student loans until my final year if you applied for one. Instead, many students including myself were provided with grants to live on. Also, because of my impairment, I also received a top up in terms of Income Support, as well as Disability Living Allowance, which my mother transferred to be paid directly to myself now I was at university. This meant that for the few years for my adult life, I had all the money I needed with very few bills and no debts.

My course was Manufacturing and Business Studies, a 3 year course with an one year placement. I wanted to do business studies as a degree although I did not have the grades for this, and I liked the atmosphere of the university as this was more than about getting a degree, this was about getting a life. I therefore liked the business specific modules although I learnt to distaste the manufacturing and especially the engineering modules. Bizarrely engineering became my least favourite subject ever, which was odd as I usually find so many other things interesting.

Some of the course was also not as accessible as they could have been, and there was quite an ad-hoc approach to trying to meet my accessible needs. This is a polite way of saying that at times my personal tutor and course leaders did not really have a clue what they were doing with myself in terms of meeting my needs. Since my days at school, I was now used to not fitting into the system and having to take a proactive role in sorting issues out related to meeting my specific needs.

One of the main difficulties for the course overall was the fact I could not draw by hand. This meant I did not do the fundamental design module in the first year, which had a significant knock on effect on other modules in the 2nd and final year. This meant there was a lot of ad-hoc adjustments needed to how I participated into the course.

But for me, I was happy doing the course however much I did not enjoy it because doing the degree paid the rent that enabled me to leave home and take part in a wide range of opportunities the university and the wider community could offer me. Very early on at University I became heavily involved in the students' union and I feel in many ways I learnt more from my activities in the union than I did from my degree.

In the November of my first year at University there was a by-election for the 'students with disabilities' officer which I stood for unopposed. This was a non-sabbatical role which I held for over 3 years, making me the union's representative on impairment issues, as well as a director of the student's union, helping with the decisions involved in running its services.

I believe this voluntary role gave me a better insight into my current role as a dysability consultant as well as developing my interest and understanding of the sociological and psychological disciplines that relate to the issue of dysability. Running my own business was merely going to be the method of my work based activities, but understanding the issues of dysability was going to be what enabled me to create real social change.

Being at university meant I had now become my own Puppet Master to my destiny away from my parents where I had more freedom with less responsibilities than I would ever have again. I loved every minute of this new-found freedom as I began my journey into becoming the person I wanted to be. I was going to make many mistakes but I was hopefully going to learn from them.

A key part of going to university that would affect the rest of my life was the need for personal assistance for my daily living activities as well as support within some of my lectures. At home with my parents, I had everything I needed assistance with in terms of my cerebral palsy within the normality of family life. Now I was living on my own, I was starting to understand what I could and could not do without assistance.

While I arrived at university with no support organised, by my second term I had organised live-in support arranged with a guy some of the other dysabled students in the Halls of Residence were using. So, in the first year I have 2 live-in personal assistants called Vicky and Joanne which mostly worked well. By the second year I had taken over managing my personal assistants myself.

This was the start of what remained a significant part of my life, employing and managing my own personal assistants. It was not always easy, and there were plenty of ups and downs over the years that is a journey for another chapter.

While most students go to University but actually still live with their parents during the holidays, visiting them as much as possible, I began the process to moving to Coventry as soon as I could. During the first two years, when I was living in the Halls of Residence, I went home as little as possible, enjoying my time with my family less and less.

By the second summer I was determined not to spend the whole summer with my parents. I ended up staying with a lecturer who I had made very good friends with, who lived in the Halls of Residence on the 18th floor, which had a wonderful view of Coventry. This was going to be most ad hoc time in my life before I settled down into a place of my own.

My course included a one year placement as the 3rd year. I did not want a placement in an engineering or manufacturing placement since I would not find it interesting nor useful to my future career. This meant that I had to enlist another department in the university to assist me with finding a placement. There was talk of a placement with a disability organisation in Oxford although it fell through.

Not disturbed by this failure to find a placement, I decided to have a year out and stay in Coventry, using the time to move and settle into my own flat. I knew that to get Housing Benefit, I needed to move away from the University and University accommodation. Unaware of social housing, I looked and found a private furnished flat on the Stoney Stanton Road, the same road I found myself back in 20 years later.

The flat was grotty looking back but it suited my needs at that time. The fact it was a decision I made and enacted myself, arranging help from friends and family was important as I believe many people with my level of impairment back then, and even now, simply do not have that level of autonomy without a lot of influence from others.

I spent my year out attending as many dysability related conferences as I could and begin the task of networking with many of the people I would be working with in the future. I always tried to get free places at conferences although I spent a lot of my own money travelling the country in an era long before the existence of social networks.

I was beginning to see where my work was going to be and this made returning to the course for the final year very difficult. I had never really enjoyed the course and now the work was really being piled on, I was not really very motivated. In the winter of the final year in a crisis of conscience I seriously considered giving up the degree because it had little relevance to what I wanted to do afterwards. In the end I finally saw sense, understanding there was no point wasting the few years' work and so I continued and finished my degree.

I left Coventry University as a graduate with a third class BSc with honours in Manufacturing and Business studies. These were the end of my days as a full-time academic student and now it was time to become a student of life and look towards making a meaningful contribution.

11 Business gain, family lost

After finishing university, I remained in Coventry and I moved to a 1 bedroom council flat in the Radford area of the city, Sadler Road. My priority was to fulfil my lifelong dream and set up my own business. I did not want to formally launch my business until I felt that I could sustain a decent income from it. I therefore spent 2 years building up my ideas and my network.

During this period, I remained on income support as I explored as much support as I could to run my business effectively. I firstly went on a NVQ Level 3 course in business ownership run by Enterprise Link, a part of Business Link in Coventry. This gave me more practical knowledge in running my own business in a manner my degree had not, and so it was indeed very helpful.

The main purpose of my business idea was to help people with impairments by providing business related consultancy on how organisations could become more accessible to people with a range of impairments. I was going to cash on the enactment of the Disability Discrimination Act 1995 to incentivised businesses to employ me. This was the plan anyway.

In 1997, Coventry University had started a Graduate Enterprise scheme that aimed to assist graduates like myself to set up their own businesses in the guise of innovation using regeneration funding from the government. I was part of the first cohort to receive funding despite the fact my idea did not exactly fit the technology focus of the other businesses, but I have never let something like this stop me.

As a condition of the funding I had to set up as a limited company and be seen to pay myself a decent wage. And so, in November 1998, Enable Enterprises Limited was born. The business name came from the fact that the aim of the business was to enable enterprises to better understand the needs of people with impairments.

On reflection, setting up as a limited company was probably not the best way forward and I would have been better to use the funding to start smaller and build up slower. Paying an accountant every year was costly if nothing else. I was being encouraged to have an office within the University's Technocentre, which thankfully never happened as it has always been better for me to work at home to meet my needs and to be more effective with my energy.

So at age 24, I had my own company within a cutting edge field. I referred to myself as a disability consultant, which was a slight bluff at that time as I was still learning the ropes. There were and remain few consultants in the field and I had to learn my role myself, being open and aware to new ideas and thinking.

I feel looking back that it was brave of myself to embark on running my own business straight from university as oppose to getting a job first, but it was something that I always wanted to do. Over the next 2 decades, my work would have many ups and downs as this story will explain further, never providing me with financial stability I have always wanted. But I have never stopped trying and over the years, I have earned the respect of many people for me around the world.

As well as setting up my business, my time after graduating from university was spent settling into my home and new hometown of Coventry as a full citizen as oppose to being just a visiting student. This primarily meant my social care and support, which I had some assistance with at university, was now being funded by Coventry City Council as oppose to West Sussex County Council, a working relationship I would now have for the rest of my life.

The more I settled I became in Coventry the further away I appeared to become from my family. Now I worked for myself I could go and visit my family when I wanted and this was less and less. I felt I had to go and see by family because that was the right thing to do. I rarely spent more than a few days with them without ending up in some kind of argument over nothing. I too often just spent the time during my stay counting the hours until I could go home, hoping to avoid the nasty side of my mother. I still have an almost weekly occurring dream of staying with parents and wanting to escape, ended up in a very angry conflict with my family.

While my real brother, Richard, stayed in Horsham, my parents spent several years moving around firstly within Horsham, then to Scotland in Glasgow and the Highlands, and finally to Spain. I am convinced my mother did not like people and tried step by step to isolate herself from others as she seemed to have a dislike for people in general. After a year or so in Spain, my mother and step-dad split up with my step-dad returning to Glasgow. The further away they became, we more we grew apart until our relationship became almost nothing.

I found it interesting and disappointing that my step father, who I had always called Brian, was very much a 'dad' when I was growing up, and a good one minus his violent outbursts, did not continue having contact with myself after splitting from my mother. I believed we had some kind of connection but that did not seem to be the case.

The last time I visited my mother in Spain was around 2000, bringing my own personal assistant with me. These few days were hell for me and I vowed it would be the last time that I would visit her. We met a few times after that in the UK and then we had minimal contact until 2009 when it ceased or at least until she friended me on Facebook very recently, simply because she had a new tablet.

My family's involvement in my story ends here. Maybe as a child and certainly as an adult, my achievements and how I have become is from my own efforts and determination with very little if any assistance from my family. I may have received my needs as a child met as a part of family life, but that does not mean they supported me in my personhood. They knew very little about me and certainly how I am now.

So, as my business ideas began to grow as my independent working life started, the involvement of my family in my life ceased for the most part. I was now very much my own person, taking responsibility for all my actions good and bad, and the resulting consequences in the ups and downs, achievements and disappointments that was going to be the rest of my life.

12 Embracing the water baby

Right before I could remember and certainly at a very early age, I loved swimming and anything to do with being emerged in water. I have always found swimming and many other water based activities enjoyable and simply pure fun. My perfect day would always include some kind of water based activity and has always featured as a part of a successful holiday.

Before I went to Forest Boys, I swam on a regular basis at school from when I went to the QE2. This meant that swimming automatically became a part of my life right from the start. While it was provided as a part of the curriculum as a form of therapy, it was something that I really enjoyed. Apparently by the time I left Southgate I could swim unaided although it was short-lived and throughout the rest of my swimming career I would need some sort of swimming aid.

While I was at Forest Boys, I did not have access to regular swimming until I joined the Sunbeam Swimming Club in 1988. Based in Horsham, this was a dysability specific club that ran on a Friday night. The club has an informal as opposed to a competitive feel, and it is quickly become an important part of my social life, as well as an opportunity to swim regularly.

Despite being just 16, my enthusiasm meant I was invited onto the club's executive committee, helping to play an active role in the running of the club. This was my first taste of the working life that I would one day have. Amongst many activities, I assisted the club to rewrite its constitution to fit into the current needs of the club. The club also gave me the opportunity to talk to many people, mainly adults, about my ideas and my dreams, and to develop my social skills.

As well as the Sunbeam Swimming Club, Horsham District Council had set up a weekly sport session for people with impairments called Ready and Able club at Christ's Hospital, a private school just outside Horsham. These sessions offered many sporting opportunities including trampolining and of course swimming. This meant that by the time I was ready to leave Horsham to go to University, I was swimming twice a week.

While I was at University, the city's swimming pool was just opposite the Halls of Residence and so I did not hesitate to continue swimming mostly alone. I also quickly found out from some of the other dysabled students about Cerebral Palsy Sport, a national sporting body for athletes for people with cerebral palsy.

A part of their activities included running regional and national swimming galas solely for people with cerebral palsy that included some races for people who used floatation devices like myself, which was fantastic. The Sunbeam swimming club's national governing body, National Association of Swimming Clubs for the Handicapped (a title I hated) did not allow people who used floatation devices to enter their competitions.

I was therefore excited at the opportunity to compete and I did exceptionally well, winning all my events at a regional and national level for a number of years. Because of my success, I was invited to take part in the cerebral palsy national team swimming squad training weekends, which was hard but enjoyable. However, people who used floatation devices could not swim internationally at any event, including the Paralympic games, and so my competitive swimming career was left stunted due to the politics of the sport.

By 1997, my competitive swimming days were over and I continued to swim as my main form of sport based leisure indefinitely. Whenever I travelled I would always take my swimming kit and try to fit in a spot of swimming somewhere as a form of second nature. My idea time for swimming would be before breakfast when I would be full of energy and because it is always better not to swim on a full stomach.

As a child, my swimming kit was very straight forward, just speedos, trunks or shorts and a towel. The only addition item would be a floatation device. If I was travelling light, this would be simply some arm bands (water wings) although I always preferred some kind of jacket to provide me full support in the water.

Over the years I tried a whole number of floatation devices as innovations and fashions have changed, and I have helped in the design of three floatation jackets. The first one was the Bubble Jacket in the late 1980s. This was made from large Bubble wrap formed into a vest shape with a crotch piece. The jacket was comfortable when it was new but like normal bubble wrap, the bubbles slowly burst as it was worn and so it ended up being useless.

The second jacket was the Swimfriends Jacket, which came with a matching floatation helmet as well as other devices. This was thick a heavy bright yellow jacket that was quite heavy and awkward to put on for me, yet alone anyone with a more severe impairment. In terms of the design, I assisted by helping to design the crotch strap to stop the jacket riding up on the body.

The final jacket was the Konfidence Jacket in the late 1990s. This was a jacket made from neoprene that was much more flexible than the Swimfriends Jacket. The jacket had foam blocks sown into lining which could be removed according to people's 'confidence'. Again, my input with the design related to the crotch strap.

Nowadays, I tend to use a standard lifejacket so long as it has a crotch strap. While I know crotch straps are not always popular I have found that are an essentially part of keeping me safe and in the jacket.

When I started competing when I was 18, I started using swimming hats, at first to simply look the part. I started with latex caps, which were very thin and uncomfortable, before moving onto thicker more comfortable silicones ones. The more I wore them, the more I realised how useful they were. They helped to keep my hair dry and my head warmer, and so my body, or that is how it felt. They make it easier to see me in the pool and so on. I liked the wide range of bright and colourful hats you could get and so I started a large collection of swimming hats from around the world which I still have today. I personally believe swimming hats should be compulsory for everyone in UK public swimming pools like in many other countries because it is more hygienic.

The next item that I added to my swimming kit was latex verruca socks. While it may seem an odd choice to use them as a preventative measure, especially as they are not very popular, especially with adults, and a pain to put on, but they worked for me. Before I used them, I used to get terrible athletes foot in my toes which I have never had since!

As my continence became an issue, I also started to wear reusable swimming nappies on their own, with shorts or with other garments. The final part of my swimming kit, other than a towel, was some kind of shorty wetsuit, rash vest or similar kind of garment. As I grow older, I become less tolerant to the cold of the water and so I started to wear something extra to keep me warm before it was fashionable to do so. With all extra kit I never minded what I looked like in the pool so long as I felt safe and comfortable.

While swimming was my main activity I also loved doing a wide range of watersports, and as I always say, anything that involved a wetsuit. My first water based activity was canoeing which I did a few times as a teenager and while I was at University. This was followed by waterskiing, jetskiing and much more as the list grew, I would and still have a go at anything at once.

Since I was more prone to the cold I was always prepared to have my own kit so I would wear a suit thicker than the activity may provide as well as having a range of accessories like booties and hoods. As my activities were so varied and with the advantage of having eBay to purchase second hand goods, I built up quite a collection of wetsuits and accessories to suit any activity in any weather condition. My favourite design of wetsuit is the old fashion two-piece beavertail type with waist pants and a jacket with a crotch piece (the beavertail) with metal fastenings, which I find very cosy and more practical.

So being a water baby with swimming and other water based activities is what has made me the happiest in myself with many fond memories over many years, with the pictures to prove it!

13 Sexual awareness

It would be wrong to talk about the journey without mentioning my sexuality and my sexual discoveries and exploits. This chapter is not going to be too graphic but it is going to be a frank discussion on what has become a blurred subject matter for me.

I think I better start with the obvious questions and answers whenever someone talks about impairment and sex. Yes, I am fully functioning down below and yes, I do have a sexual appetite in my own non-traditional way. While it is not always appropriate to ask, I prefer people ask these kinds of questions so they get it off their mind, and hopefully by being open about it myself, I am allowing other people with impairments to have a level of privacy I never had.

My sexuality was something I did not really consider until my early 20s. In my teens, a period of desiring normality, I had the usual expectations of getting married, having children, being rich and having a nice big house. I however think not much more about it as I was too busy getting an education and coping with the everyday challenges that I was facing. As a teenager, I can confirm that my sexual urges were developing in the normal way and I was able to manage them.

Coming out to myself about my sexuality was not a gradual process but rather a sudden one. I was 21 and it was Christmas Day in 1995, I was at home with my family for one of those 'lets pretend we are happy' lunches. My younger real brother and older step brother, was there both acting the fool in that lads' culture I hadnever really liked. I just looked at them and suddenly thought to myselfI am not like them, so therefore I must be gay!

The revelation was very comforting to me as it all made sense. Everything else in my life was unusual and complex, so why not my sexuality? Over the next year I became more comfortable and confident with my identity and I fully came out with my student union peers at NUS National Conference in Blackpool that Easter. In 2005 I would really come out in a big way in a front page on the Guardian in an advert for the charity Scope.

I would never hide the fact I am gay, but neither would you I rub it into someone's face. I don't particularly look kemp in the traditional sense but I do think my behaviour and mannerisms within the boundaries of my uncoordinated movements show some of my gayness. I have always enjoyed the opportunity to attend Gay Pride events in London, Birmingham and just recently Coventry. I really like going to London Pride because there is always a 'safe space' for people with impairments in the parade that is a great way to see the sights of London as well as feeling a part of something special.

I honestly believe I have not experienced any direct or even indirect homophobia that I am aware of. I believe one reason for this is that because I have a significant impairment that has occupied the majority of my identity and political space, my identity as someone who is gay has been smaller and less significant to me as compared to someone who is gay without a significant impairments This does not mean I believe being gay is less important but simply it is something I had less time for in terms of my political identity.

The other side of my sexuality is my sex exploits. I have never found the idea of any intercourse interesting although I do enjoy masturbating, which is as crude as this chapter gets. My interests are rather based on fetishes and I have plenty of them which relates to many aspects of my lifestyle.

I decided after much deliberation that I would not go into a whole list of my fetishes as I feel it will distract from the story and messages I am attempting to portray. I am not ashamed of any of my fetishes which are all harmless and do not involve others in any real way, but I do not see the need to be excessively open about them. Those who know myself and my lifestyle will either know or be able work out what my fetishes may be.

What I can say is that my fetishes can be generally seen in terms of a desire to feel safe, protected and at times, dependent. The latter is particularly significant because I have believed for many years that some of my fetishes have been important in balancing my life and emotional wellbeing. Due to the many impairment related barriers I have faced by insisting on participating within mainstream society, I have needed to become over-independent and therefore my fantasies needed to assist me to counteract this.

I have been able to build many of my fetishes into the way I live in a natural way, often because I find the item useful in terms of their intended usage in a real context which has nothing to do with being sexual, but rather just how I wish to live. I have always found the psychologically behind this very interesting, especially when I share my experiences with other people with significant impairments, particularly those with cerebral palsy.

The final thing to mention on the matter is my alter-ego, Frank, who is more physically and mentally dependent than myself. Frank is a part of me which few people will ever see and someone I may use in role plays. Again, I believe that the natural creation of Frank has been born from my over-independence, and a need to sometimes let go of being in control, which has been something I have found difficult to do.

I am generally comfortable about my sexuality and I am happy with my endeavours in the what has so-far been quite a small part of my life compared to my other endeavours.

14 Becoming myself

During my early 20s, as well as setting up my own business, my focus in this stage of myself was to explore how to develop myself, to become the best version of myself. There were a number of activities that I took part is which I believe greatly contributed to myself becoming a better person and also becoming myself, whoever that was.

The first activity was that I purchased and listened to a lot of personal development and self-improvement tapes. Not only did these many tapes give me a better understanding of myself and my place within the world, but it also gave me a better understanding of the personal development in developing the notion of personal responsibility in myself and others.

I found the tapes really useful and I put what I was learning to practise as opposed to simply becoming addicted to the tapes, which can be the problem with a lot of self-help solutions, like Alcoholics anonymous. The tapes laid down a commitment to be as organised in my work and personal activities as I can in order to go that extra mile to achieve what I wanted in life.

The second activity that helped me being myself was my participation in three working holidays organised by an organisation called Choice. The aim was for undergraduates to volunteer their time to primarily support young people from poorer backgrounds to be inspired to go to university. It is important to understand that I was the only impaired volunteer in these projects, which was an achievement in itself.

The first project was in the summer of 1993 in Aberystwyth, at the University. I was part of a team of undergraduates that were supporting pupils in Liverpool on a week's residential course exploring their goals for their future. It was hard work, long hours but really enjoyable and rewarding to do. I realised that helping others find themselves helped me find myself. The week also had one of the amusing moments I can remember because the university was built on a hill, when I arrived and asked where the lift was, the answer was upstairs!

Built on the success of taking part in this project, I applied for a bigger project with Choice the following year. This time it was a 6 weeks period to teach English to many young people at Kings College in Lagos, Nigeria! This was a very different affair which is a long story in itself. Basically, we arrived just after the country has had an election and there was complete and utter mayhem in a manner that would be unimaginable in this country. Basically, with the bank closed and the electricity cut for most day, we were living and working in primitive conditions where anything that could go wrong did go wrong.

I found the whole project immensely challenging on many levels and I had to do a lot of soul searching in order to get through the project for the time I was there, after a week staying at the college, I became ill with gastroenteritis and spent most of the following week in hospital. I sadly decided that for my physical and emotional health, I had to leave after 2 weeks, and it took me many months to recover emotionally during a period I did not know I had mild bipolar. With all this said, I still enjoyed the project on reflection, especially in terms of the friendships I made, and what I gave to the project. I certainly have no regrets about going to Nigeria.

In 1996, when I had finished my degree, I decided to do one last project with Choice during the summer as this would be potentially the last time I could afford to have a long period away without having a knock on effect with what would be my growing responsibilities. This time it was six weeks in Prague. As soon as all the undergraduates and graduates had arrived the original project had collapsed.

While we had our accommodation and food for the period in place, it was up to us to create the project ourselves. Some of the volunteers stuck with the original idea of teaching English while others simply used the time for sightseeing across Eastern Europe. A large proportion of the volunteers including myself decided to do something a bit different and put on a very adapted multilingual version of Romeo and Juliet in the middle of Prague's Old Town Square on their national monument.

The performance grew into something quite huge. It was more than a simple piece of street theatre with people watching for a few minutes before moving on, this be a full blown unofficial invasion of talent. We had to get permission from the deputy mayor of the city, who organised for area we were performing in to be cleared. I played the middle of three versions of Romeo as well as having a large role in writing and directing of the play in what was a chaotic democracy, I was maybe one of a handful of people who understood the full meaning of the play.

What I really liked about Prague was that it came me a lot of confidence with commuting around a city on a daily basis and exploring things for myself. I also built up a lot of strong friendships from the experience, including Petra, a very good professional dancer from Prague. He visited me in the UK that winter and I visited him the following year.

My involvement in the third and greatest activity to develop my personhood literally started for me straight after my time in Prague. This was European Human Bridges or EHB, an informal project run by trainers across Europe to bring young people with and without impairments throughout the continent to week long to ten day seminars each year focusing on personal development and intercultural learning.

I became involved with EHB through meeting one of the UK trainers on canal boat in Coventry. The first project was in Levoca in Slovakia, so the UK team of trainers and participants met in Prague before getting a train to Bratislava to meeting everyone else before going by coach to Levoca.

Levoca was the first of many projects, others were held in Stockholm in Sweden, Lake Balaton in Hungary, Saravero in Bosnia, Strasbourg in France, Mamia in Romania and Izmir in Turkey. The projects were funded by both Council of Europe and European Union monies as a part of their youth programmes. While I was a participant for the first two years, I then became one of the trainers and organisers, taking a lead role in developing the philosophy of the project overall.

EHB was very important to me and how I developed as a person. These were very enjoyable and hard working seminars with lots of alcohol and little sleep. I found them very intense and quite an emotional rollercoaster at times. Learning with young people with and without impairments from so many different cultural backgrounds, whether as participants or trainers, was so amazing and probably where I have learnt the most in my life.

The motto of the project was making the impossible possible, which has now become my own motto, because this is what we did. EHB was not any form of formal organisation but simply a collection of trainers volunteering to come together once a year, as well as preparation and evaluation meetings, to do a seminar to make a difference to other people. When things went wrong, as they very often did, we found a way of solving the problem together. It was a spirit I really valued and I feel is often missing in today's impairment politics.

As a result of my work with EHB, I was able to take part in many youth, human rights, and equality related conferences organised by the Council of Europe at one of their youth centres in Strasbourg and Budapest. In the name and spirit of EHB, I meant my own unique impact and I am proud to have had the opportunity to make a difference in little ways at an European level, offering a positive viewpoint on impairment issues.

While there were many other smaller activities that helped me become myself, these were the top three. I believe personal development is something no one should stop working towards as there is always something more we can learn about ourselves and our relationships with others. Writing this story has been a new exercise itself in finding out who I am by exploring my past and time will tell how that has.

15 Loving Coventry

Coventry has been my home since September 1992 when I came to University. A lot of people I have met over the years from Coventry said they did not like the city, but I have always loved the city for many reasons. As I have become more settled, the more it became a place that I felt that I would never want to leave from as my home and base for my travels, unless there was a really significant incentive to move away like a huge salary offer.

The first thing I love about Coventry is its location. The city in right is the middle of the country and just 20 minutes from Birmingham by road and by rail. It has very look links to the motorway both north and south as well as very good connections on the railway network. London is only 1 hour away on Virgin Trains, and it is possible to make a day trip by train to many cities and towns across the country, and even Paris or Brussels by Eurostar.

The only downside to the city's location is that it is nowhere near the seaside or any beaches in any direction, all of which are hours away by car or train. As someone who loves watersports, I miss that constant access to that surfing culture, where everyone from new-born to grandma owns a wetsuit! Often on holiday I love just sitting on a beach in a wetsuit and booties simply breathing and letting thoughts wash over me.

Another thing I like about Coventry is that it is a mostly compact city. By this I mean that from the city centre, it is easy to get to the open countryside within 15 minutes by car in any direction. This means you can enjoy the benefits of urban living as well as the quiet countryside with nice pubs serving good food and other interesting places to visit. Coventry is very near Stratford-upon-Avon, which is the birthplace of William Shakespeare and a very nice place to visit in the summer.

The downside is while public transport is very good within the boundaries of Coventry, the bus services around the wider Warwickshire are very limited and lengthy. It is often easier to get to

Birmingham or even London than it is to get to places within Warwickshire especially if you do not have a car. While the buses are good and now fully accessible in Coventry, all the routes go via the city centre, making crossing the city often time consuming.

A final thing I like about Coventry is that with the infamous inner ring road there is a clear and mostly pedestrianised city centre full of shops and restaurants. Admittedly the lure of the centre has waned over the last decade or so, although there has recently been a lot of regeneration work being carried out in centre of Coventry, making the future of area look bright.

I am lived in six places in Coventry including my time at the university. I have mostly lived in the north of the city, although I have recently moved to a lovely place very near the city centre. This has meant where I used to go shopping and to restaurants within my local suburb, I have now found a new appreciation for the city centre.

I have believed for many years in investing time and effort in my local community in terms of local services whether they are commercial, voluntary or statutory. This means if I see something wrong with a service I regularly use in a large or small way, then I would politely inform the service of my concerns. It is amazing how I would often be the first person to inform them of something very obvious like a missing road sign.

My attitude is by helping my local community in this way I am helping myself in ensuring the things in my everyday life that could reduce the small element of stress we face when things are not as they should be. And it works, over the years I have put so many things right in Coventry in small ways that many people would not notice.

By my mid-20s, I was certainly settled in Coventry, working every hour I had available to try to secure a stable income, as well as ensuring I had a lot of fun on the way. While I saw Coventry as a home, that did not mean I stopped travelling around the country and indeed the country. However, now I had work to do and other commitments, I could now only afford to go away for a maximum of 2 weeks at a time like most of my peers. However much I loved going away on relaxing and working breaks, I always also looked forward to coming home to all my creature comforts.

I know that wherever I would have ended up settling I would feel positive about although I do not believe you should spend much time thinking what if and how life would be or indeed is in the infinite parallel universes if you believe in that sort of thing as I often wonder. I am sure that if Coventry had not felt right for me by the time I had left university, I would have moved somewhere else, probably London.

There have been a couple of times where I have consider moving to London. The advantage would be that I would be closer to many of my customers from over the years, and I would have more opportunities to attend the many nationally relevant work related networking days and evening events without the time and cost of travelling to London. However, I realised that moving to London would very unlikely result in being able to live in 'Zone 1' and that it was actually often quickly for me to get home to Coventry from events than it was for people who were living in London. This realisation has kept me from wishing further to move to London as well as the enormous stress such a decision would bring.

So, Coventry has now been my home for half my life and I intend to stay here for the rest of my life however long that may be. It may not be a perfect city but it is the place I call home.

16 Needing support

One of the largest impairment related activities in my life has been the employment and management of personal assistants. A personal assistant in the context of social care is someone who is directly employed by a person with an impairment to support them with the things they find difficult so they live in the way they choose. Personal assistants are not carers or care workers, who often work for someone else and delivery support according to the care plan prescribed by the funding body that is paying for the support.

I think at this stage is it important to understand how my main impairment, cerebral palsy, affects me on a daily basis. Basically, the severity of my impairments affects the way I do everything and I need support in many of the activities I need to do each day to keep my alive and running as a fully contributing citizen.

This includes getting dress, preparing meals, cutting up food, washing up, laundry, hoovering, cleaning, shaving and the lists goes on. I am not completely dependent like some other people requiring support or in the way you may expect but my needs are varied and significant enough to become a dominating issue in my life.

A lot of what I need is not specifically about what I can or cannot do but rather about having limited energy each day and having to decide what to do myself and what to get assistance with. Since my personal assistants are unlikely to be able to do my own work on my behalf, this is something that I must prioritise while they assist me with housework and other activities.

My assistance was for many years funded by 3 organisations; the local authority, Independent Living Fund (ILF), and Department of Work Access to Work scheme. In July 2015, ILF closed and the funding was transferred to the local authority. While the way I have social care funding from 3 funders is technically called an Individual Budget, it remains quite unusual to have had support from all 3 funders.

The reason I have needed to apply for support from 3 funders as oppose to just one is because none of the funders would be able to support all my needs. This is because the different funders have different eligibility criteria with different ways of assessing people. This means that every year or so I have had 3 different assessments and reviews in 3 different ways using 3 different sets of rules and 3 different sets of expectations, which I have needed to fit my single life and needs into.

When you start to employ personal assistants, who are then dependent on you for their wages, these assessments can often come along unannounced and this can be quite stressful. Those assessing myself simply see the assessment in terms of my needs and they are often very unaware of the emotional impact of what they are doing, and the level of stress these assessments can cause. But assessments have always been a part of getting the funding I need for my support, and I will always be at the mercy of assessments through ever changing policies and practices for the rest of my life.

Now we come at the heart of something that remains critical to my life; directly employing and managing personal assistants. The first thing I am always asked in this respect is whether I actually do employ my personal assistants, which is an assumption that maybe they are actually working for someone else. Like it or not, I do directly employ them in the same way as any employer would employ staff. I am therefore responsible for every aspect of their employment and their rights as an employee in the same way as anyone else.

The interesting point is when I started to employ my own personal assistants at aged 19, I had no training or experience. I had to learn my responsibilities as well as the aspects of inter-personal management from scratch with very little support from others. This has meant that I have made a lot of mistakes in a lot of ways which I have learnt from, developing my own unique understanding on the subject. This is why I have recently produced a comprehensive guide for others on how to employ personal assistant called Understand Support, so they can learn from my mistake and maybe avoid making some of them themselves.

I have lost count of how many personal assistants I have employed since I started. I have recruited people from all ages and backgrounds, some have lasted many years while others have literally lasted a few hours or days. My longest serving personal assistant is also my current and best one, Flora, who has worked for me for over ten years and we have kept a strong relationship throughout that time.

When I recruit staff, the important qualities I am looking for are good communication and a positive attitude. Anyone should be able to do the physicality's of the work as that is reasonably simple. However, if they can not communicate well with me, or they are unwilling to see me as the boss who is able to take responsibility for his actions, including the actions that affects them, than the relationship will breakdown very quickly.

Employing a complete stranger to support you in your own home and asking them to do often very intimate tasks can be very daunting. It is important you are and feel safe with your personal assistant and so I have developed a collection of policies and practises which I refer to as active safeguarding. This means that I routinely perform activities to keep me safe.

An example of this would be I often send my staff to the shops on my behalf to purchase items with my debit or credit card using a pin number or contactless payment. I am upfront about the fact I check my bank and other accounts online each day and so I would know about any unauthorised activities, and everyone is also aware I would not hesitate to involve the police if that was appropriate.

This is a relationship where trust is a complex issue. It is possible to trust personal assistants to a point but at the same time you need to have a plan for when circumstances, deliberate or otherwise, means they let you down. I have learnt the hard way that for every situation, you need a Plan B, C, D, E and so on. I think this is the way I generally think as I am unwilling to allow anyone or anything from stopping me from doing anything that I wish to do.

Over the years, I have had a lot of personal assistants try to and at times succeed in abusing me. In late 1999, I had one very young personal assistant literally run away with my bank card and PIN number, stealing £3700 through cashpoint machines over the millennium New Year period before I discovered what he had done and could involve the police. He was never caught and luckily my bank agreed to repay me the money.

Employing personal assistants can be a lot of work and when it goes wrong, it can be extremely stressful and disheartening. There have been times when I have been recruiting every few weeks because I have not found people suitable for my requirements. It can also be hard to balance what you are unwilling to compromise on and what you are prepared to make do with.

When the relationship between myself and my personal assistants have worked well, it has been amazing. A good personal assistant will learn what I need each day without me having to explain every time. They will also be someone I will be comfortable chatting with, telling them what is on my mind, and therefore supporting my emotional needs as well as my physical ones. They would also hopefully put me in a good state of being so that I am able to move forward in the goals of my life with more speed than if I was unhappy with my support.

My relationship with my personal assistants can sometimes feel like a marriage in many respects as you can be spending a lot of time with them. Like a marriage, it can be a firm and stable relationship that can last for years, or it can quickly into a disaster with a very messy and painful divorce.

Employing personal assistants is a lifelong commitment which most people without significant impairments are never likely to experience, a whole job comparable to parenting. I hope my extensive experience will support me better in the ups and downs of my future support where it is certain that all my staff are always going to leave at some point.

As well as employing personal assistants, since 2008 I have been using lived-in volunteers from Voluntary Matters, which will be discussed further in another chapter. The balance of employing personal assistants and having lived-in volunteers have provided me with a very stable and rewarding support package in recent years that I hope will continue.

17 Denormalisation

When I was in my teens it was just automatic for me to feel that I had to be as normal as possible in everything I did. I remember each New Year I would resolve to use a knife and fork for meals, as opposed to a spoon, which was simply last a few days or weeks before reverting back to normal. I did not felt at all pressured to be normal as it is simply the environment I was in.

In my late teens and early 20s, I become to explore what I would like to use or could use on a daily basis in a manner that would better met my impairment needs, often just in terms the use of basic equipment, in a way that would not be seen as not normal. As well as myself, I seen many other people with cerebral palsy go through this process at around the same age as myself, and I now refer to the process as denormalisation, which is a kind of second adolescence that many people with cerebral palsy experience, particularly if they went to a mainstream school.

The first issue I approached was the use of some kind of mealtime protection as I did often make a mess when I was eating. Before my teens I used to wear old terry towel nappies as bibs but I stopped as a teen. I looked at a wide range of options from simple bibs, to plastic smocks with sleeves to full boilersuits. My exploration meant that I built up quite a collective of mealtime protectors over the years, as I did with every issue I explored.

This is when I began to realise that it was not about having one solution but rather a range of solutions to suit different situations, and that lifestyle was about making complex choices that no one else had to understand. Nowadays I tend to mostly wear a neoprene bib all the time if I am at home or just for mealtimes when I am out. If I really want to look my best before a meal, then I may wear a plastic smock with sleeves so I am fully covered.

The challenge with wearing that could be seen as something different is overcoming what you may perceive other people to think about it.

The reality is others will mostly simply see what you decide to use as simply something you need because of your impairments, especially if they have always seen you use that piece of equipment. I however do feel that the irrational fear of what others may think does stop some people from making changes to their lifestyle that could bring them practical benefits.

The second issue I explored was my posture when I am sitting, particularly in terms of being in a wheelchair or vehicle seat. While I could walk most of the time until my mid-30s and I am still able to walk at home, I have never been a stranger to a wheelchair throughout my life for one reason or another. My sitting posture could always be better and so I looked at ways to assist it in terms of using harnesses.

Like with mealtime protection, I have tried a lot of harnesses with mix success. I have never liked the modern butterfly style harnesses most people with cerebral palsy end up using, as I prefer the more traditional five point harnesses since having a crotch strap stops me from sliding down the seat if properly fastened. The problem is that these kinds of harnesses can be they are complex to fasten, especially since they are almost impossible to keep untangled.

If a seat on a minibus has a harness on it in my late teens and beyond, which I now appreciated as opposed to my days at school, I would always try to wear it even if that involved a great deal of untangling. This was about personal choice and a desire to use things that made me feel good about myself in ways that was often very hard to explain.

The next issue I explored was my continence and particularly the use of nappies. I use the term nappies since I hate the term 'pads' and like a lot of people with lifelong impairments, I have always been proud about using nappies. Apart from a period when I was very ill, I have never been fully incontinent although there have been times where I have had accidents because I have not reached the toilet in time. I also tend to slightly leak urine after I have been to the toilet.

These issues have meant that wearing nappies have been an useful precaution when I go out and enables me to feel safe and comfortable as oppose to anything else. Because of the way I thrust my hips when I walk I discovered that this made my nappies prone to gradually falling off, so I started to use plastic pants over them to keep them secure, which duly solved the problem. With a lot of my lifestyle choices, it was a matter of trail and error.

The most significant lifestyle choice I made to my personhood and my whole identity was starting to wear a helmet all the time when I go out. The idea started when I was 17 at Collyer's when one icy day I slipped on some black ice. I must had knocked myself out as I do not remember hitting the ground. This experience planted the seeds of the idea, especially when I started University and was considering getting around the campus in the winter.

While I started with an off-the-shelf watersports helmet that I only used in the winter months, it was not long before I managed to acquire free NHS helmets in a range of colours that were more appropriate for my needs on a long-term basis. These scrum style leather covered helmets were designed for people with epilepsy and headbangers, as well as people with cerebral palsy and others like myself.

Gradually I wore my helmets more and more, until it was every time I went out, and it has now reached a point where I feel naked if I do not go out without a helmet. As someone always in the media and who gets photographed a lot, the helmet has become an important part of my identity and could indeed now be seen as a part of my branding. The helmet itself may be unusual but the use of headwear generally as a form of branding is not unusual.

While these are the main items I have adopted as a part of my denormalisation process, there are also many other small items I have adopted. These include special cups, wider handled cutlery and many other little things I may not even realise. It also includes my swimming and water based activity kits I have discussed previously, as well as specialist equipment for other activities like wearing a leotard and shorts for physical activities so that my nappy does not show.

A part of the denormalisation process for me has been an eagerness to try to whole range of new stuff and activities to see what I like and what I do not like, and to see what works for me. Activities have included a wide range of sports including fencing and wrestling, finger painting, and 'work experience' sessions like at a garage with mechanics. These sessions have always been about having a go and enjoying the experiences, as opposed to comparing myself with anyone else.

The process has also meant not been frightened to use things I like and find comfortable which other people may consider odd or unusual. This would include the fact that I find boilersuits and American style prison scrubs very comfortable as casual wear at home, and I now have a large collection of overalls in the design of many different manufacturers.

My exploration of many different items within the denormalisation process has been expensive at times, and thanks for the amazing variety of 'stuff' available on eBay, I have built up a large collection of often weird and wonderful items from sleep suits with back zips, to lycra Spiderman outfits to even a straitjacket!.

I liked to purchase what I wanted to find out more about it in terms of how they felt and what practical use I could find from them. Admittedly, much of what I have purchased has not been worn often as I had not found a suitable occasion for that although if I have ever invited to a fancy-dress party then I would certainly be prepared as I have enough outfits to lend to a whole football team!

The whole denormalisation process has helped me become more confident in myself and in being the person I wished to be as someone with significant impairments. It was a process that took many years and included my ability to reclaim my impairment needs from the pressures of conforming to a mainstream society. It required courage and determination to become the person I wished to be,

18 Finding my soul mate

Love was something I never looked for but it was indeed something I found naturally. I think because of the extra burdens of having an impairment, running my own business and employing my own personal assistants, I simply did not consider having an intimate relationship with anyone as there was simply no time.

I was never really into any form of dating and I was perfectly happy being a bachelor for the rest of my life. Because I knew I was gay I think I have decided against having children. This was not because I felt I could not physically have them or be able to be a good father if I wanted or needed to, but I understood that I had to be quite selfish to achieve what I was achieving in life and therefore it would have been unfair to have children.

After I came out to myself about being gay, I was maybe now in a position to consider relationships as I knew now at least what ballpark I was playing in. However, coincidence or maybe fate solved my relationship issues quickly and naturally before I had time to even embark on any meaningful exploration.

I first met Patrick when I was doing a 2nd year module in my final year of study on product development, because it interested me more than other final year modules on offer. In the module we had to design and research a product as a part of a year-long project. Our group under my lead decided to focus on impairment friendly wide handled cutlery.

A part of our research we visited and met students from Hereward College, a specialist further education college with people with impairments that I would have a lot of dealings with over the years. And so this is where I met Patrick in the winter of 1995.

Patrick has a level of cerebral palsy that is far greater than my own. He has no verbal communication and he is unable to do anything physically for himself, requiring a level of personal support that is far greater than my own. Despite all this, he is able to express himself eloquently through his facial expressions and body language, and he is one of the most independent and inspiring people I know. He can also be a total pain in the neck which is also something I love about him.

After meeting him for the first time, I saw them around university occasionally which I found confusing until I understood he was studying Applied Social Sciences at the University but that he was staying at Hereward College. For his studies, he had a volunteer to support him, Libby, and for a range of unusual coincidences, Libby ended up supporting me during the Easter holidays when I went to the NUS National Conference in Blackpool, the one where I came out as being gay. This gave me a better opportunity to find out some more about Patrick and vice-versa.

In a final turn of events, with the start of the internet becoming affordable if not still novel, I had a modem installed on my computer that also allowed me to send and receive faxes. Almost as soon as I did this I began receiving odd phone calls that ended up being a fax from Patrick inviting me to visit him.

So, in the afternoon of 6th May 1996, Patrick and I properly met at Hereward College, and for me at least it was love at first sight as I kissed him just before leaving in a way I have never kissed anyone before. From that moment, our relationship grew and grew as it was clear to me that we were soulmates.

Right for the first time I met him, I was respectful and patient to his preferred method of formal communication, which at the time was using his communication aid with head switches, as now he uses eyegazing technology. I believe I was one of the first people to talk to him as an adult and enabled him to be more confident and independent with himself, always coming up with solutions to problem in our way.

He did not always like the fact I treated him as an equal because it meant I would challenge him when I felt he was wrong in a way only his mother ever did. His mother had a big and positive influence in

Patrick's life although she was not someone you wanted to get on the wrong side of, something I often did as Patrick was never good at keeping secrets from anyone, especially his own and especially to his mother.

At the beginning of our relationship as boyfriend and boyfriend, I imagined a traditional pathway into coming together as a partnership, living together and sharing everything together like a married couple, long before we could ever consider legally being married. However, it became clear that because of our impairments and the level of social independence we had, we both had to be selfish in a positive way to achieve what we needed and wanted.

This meant that while we could always have relationship together, we needed a level of separation so we could properly manage our individual lives. Patrick had won a compensation case from the brain damage he received during his birth. This meant he purchased his own bungalow in a very nice part of Coventry, and he had the funding for his support he needed without being dependent on statutory services in the way I was. I was working my way up the financial ladder in my own way which brought its own advantages and disadvantages. This meant that because of our difference financial and living situations, it became more important that we lived separately however much we may spend time together as equals.

As well as being friends with Patrick, as well as having a sexual relationship, I also assisted Patrick with his writing his essays, or rather I wrote most of the essay for him which he paid me to do. Using his head switches meant he was a very slow typer and so it is often easier for me to write things for him. I also often became his advocate, assisting him with dealing with organisations and making complaints.

In October 2004, we separated when I was having a difficult period which is explained later in the story. Patrick refuse to speak to me for six years, I believe because of the anger and frustration he saw in me when I was having a difficult time. I probably also needed that space to sort out my problems without having to worry about him and what he thought. Patrick also had a frustrating habit of telling me what other people thought of me, particularly his personal assistants, without clarifying his own position, causing a lot of misunderstanding and mayhem at times.

In 2010 we came back together as just good friends with some benefits. We had always had a very open and relax relationship since he has a sexual appetite that I was never really interested in fulfilling, I just liked a kiss and a cuddle in bed on a lazy workday afternoon. We both loved our food and very often went out for meals together as well as a whole load of fun things that any 2 best friends would do.

I am quite an emotional and passionate person who is never afraid to say how I am feeling, while Patrick is, compared to myself, mostly very reserved about his emotions as he has his mother's stiff upper lip. This made him very much an emotional rock for me, with a level of stability and understanding about my impairment that meant I did not feel alone in that area anyway.

Patrick, like everyone, has not been able to meet all my emotional needs as they remain so diverse due to my mental health needs. There have certainly been times where Patrick simply did not know how to respond to what he saw as my emotional outbursts. Because he has little experience with dealing with emotions, his response when I felt upset was often to laugh which certainly never helped the situation.

I feel very honoured and grateful to have someone as emotionally and mentally strong in my life who I could call my soulmate. I have never met anyone who has every came close to having a relationship like I have had with Patrick, and I have never looked for anyone to replace Patrick, even when I was without him.

I feel everyone deserves to find a soulmate, someone they feel they can share their life with even if it is a non-traditional way, and I love the fact I naturally found my soulmate in life. But like any relationship, it takes work to maintain to keep alive and fresh. As we have our own separate lives, there may be weeks when Patrick and I are speaking online on Skype by text, our preferred method, a couple of times each day, and other weeks where we would simply not hear from each other knowing that we were both okay.

Having a real best friend like Patrick has helped me to feel whole, especially during the darker days of my life.

19 Bobbing along

My late 20s were a little bit blurry as I was simply bobbling along as everything was seeming to go well. I was leaving my youthful days behind as I was entering my 30s, the mainstay of my adulthood. While it is hard for me to remember everything that went on in the period, there were a number of activities that stick out for me.

The first was the fact that I attempted to do a Masters (MA) in Disability Studies at Sheffield University. I say attempted because I gave up the course half way after one year because I simply did not like the bias of the course towards psychoanalysis, a subject I could never get my head around. I was paying for the course from my own money and I did not see the point of wasting money on something that I was not enjoying.

The course was a distanced learning two year course that included an one week residential placement at the start of each year at the university. The week of lectures included around six disability studies students and was shared with 40 other psychoanalysis students on various courses. There were some lectures we did solely as disability studies students and others we did as a whole cohort.

My conclusion from the first year's week was that the majority of the psychoanalytic students were totally crazy, especially when it came to disability issues. The disability students group from both years we're made up of people with and without impairments, although I was the only one with a very obvious level of impairment. If you add in my confidence and outgoing nature, as well as my sense of humour, I clearly became a focus of attention of the psychoanalytic students as each one individually seem to decide to dump all their hang-ups about impairment issues onto me, quite literally.

During the week, I am not sure I have laugh so much before or since as it was the only way to avoid bursting into tears. The other disability studies students were extremely supportive as we laughed and joked about some of the ridiculous things that the other students were saying and doing. It certainly did not provide me with a positive picture of the next generation of psychotherapists or any respect of the subject that seemed to be to me simply a cult following of Sigmund Freud.

I did find the parts of the course which related to impairment and disability very interesting, and it did indeed broaden my understanding of the topic and appreciate how complex and diverse it was. However, I did find the restrictions of academia in terms of not coming up with new ideas difficult. My understanding of impairment and dysability issues come from a lived experience in a personal and working lives where I know things often without the ability of knowing where my knowledge has come from.

I do not regret doing the course, nor do I regret giving up the course either. The course did indeed provide me with a useful insight into the complex issues of disability that has assisted me to have the rounded understanding I have now that supports me to be a current leader in the field. But at the same time, I was not prepared to pay another £2000, a lot of money, for something I was not enjoying. I felt I had got what I wanted from this specific adventure and so I was happy.

A second activity during this period was my work as the accessibility director of 4dp.com. This website was the brainchild of Neil Allday from Burnley, and it had the potential to be the leading impairment specific website of that time. I am not quite sure how I became involved in the website, which is true of a lot of my work, which was from a measure of networking and cold emails at that time.

The website was basically a directory of products and services covering the needs of people with a range of impairments. The website was 'for disabled people' and therefore had the domain name of 4dp.com. There was a brief conversation stemming from the investors about using the term people with disabilities, making it 4pwd.com and I was called in for my expert opinion to save the day.

I was on a retainer contract of £300 a month for a year or so, with the role to designing a category system for the site, based on work I had already done for my own database of contacts. I also helped develop a relationship site called 4dp Together. Since I was the only person involved with the site with an obvious impairment, where everyone else came from a trade background, it was clear that I had an important role to play to ensure the site had a cultural awareness of all the impairment related issues.

One frustration I had with the site was that I was still living and working remotely for the site from Coventry, where the site was based in Burnley. Not only did this mean long journeys on the train to get to meetings but also it often meant I did not see what was going on from day to day. The business behind the website had employed a young website designer who I believed was not developing the site as fast as it could and should have been. I knew the site has had it day before it reached its full potential when my monthly cheque bounced!

Over the years, I would see an endless number of 'disability' websites come and go, often always optimistic about the eventual failed business models of advertising or membership fees. My observations of 4dp.com and many other websites gave me a better understanding of the internet and the rise of social media in terms of people with impairments and dysability issues.

A third activity was my own online shop using the eBay platform. Because of all the knowledge and experience I had about the benefits of people with impairments using a wide range of equipment from my denormalisation process, I decided to sell a wide of products I used myself to help other people in a similar position. I realised that it was often the little things that made the biggest difference to people's lives like pieces of equipment.

The shop sold many items including bibs, smocks with sleeves in all sizes, swimming hats, swimming socks and plastic pants. My bigger seller was swimming nappies which were in all sizes for children and adults, like many of my products. I feel people respected that I called things what they were upfront, as opposed to using 'dignity' terms in hide what things were discreetly. By this, I mean for adults with lifelong conditions, bibs and nappies did not stop being bibs and nappies now they are not children if they still need them.

I used to enjoy the relationship I would build with customers like parents and others, who would be very grateful for what my shop offered, which was often things they had been desperately looking for like swimming nappies for school swimming. While these interactions may have been small, it was nice to know that I was helping other people in important ways.

Like everything, the shop closed in 2008 for a number of reasons. It was a good experience but the profit margins was very small. As a part of my process of always reviewing my goals and outcomes, I wanted to focus on high value products and services that were not as time consuming, or dependent on the sometimes highly inefficient postal service.

My late 20s were also a time when I did a lot of leisure activities, trying out many new experiences like power-gliding as I was still discovering myself. I had a car from the Motability scheme at that time and I was making the most of it, especially during the summer months. It was a time where money seemed okay and I was managing my life generally well.

I was also doing a lot of travelling and I had the wonderful opportunity of attending a huge conference on self-directed support in Seattle with a colleague and his family, where I met many other British colleagues in the social care field who I would be working more with in the future. Just before the conference, a group of us went on a hovercraft to Victoria, British Columbia in Canada where we went Whale Watching.

My health during the period was reasonably good although I had a big problem with acid reflux, to the point I needed a successful operation on my stomach to halt what was a very uncomfortable and dangerous situation. When I went to sleep, the very second I fell asleep I would vomit up acid. This would require me to bolt up and reach the toilet as the acid went into my nose and eyes, really unpleasant stuff. As soon as I had the operation, one that most people only need in their 50s, the problem ceased although I am now still wary of eating late and lying flat in bed.

My late-20s was a period of steady growth that allowed me to have some kind of 2nd childhood before my 30s, a period of hard work I was certainly not quite prepared for after this period of bobbing along. I still had a lot to learn and a lot of growing to do as I moved from a young adult looking for recognition into a full adult fighting and eventually winning recognition from his peers and indeed many others in a way that was not possible at this time.

20 The Helen effect

The year 2004 was the year everything in my life began to change and initially not for the better although what would become a full ten-year project throughout my thirties that would eventually drag me almost kicking and screaming into a whole new level of happiness and recognition.

The year started with a phone call from Access to Work, a part of the Department of Work and Pensions, who simply asked if I received funding from the Independent Living Fund for my personal support, which was fair enough. Then about a week later I had a call from Helen Tyers, a senior social worker at the fund, suggesting that unless I could immediately prove that I was not double funding my support with the fund and Access to Work then my support funding would be stopped straight away. Her hostile tone already put my back up.

I acknowledge that I had previously not informed both parties of my other funding outside their remit because I saw them as separate entities and I knew I was not double funding my support, getting the two amounts for the same set of hours. It was a matter that could have been very easily sorted although it became something much bigger and quite damaging.

The initial problem was certainly the attitude of Helen Tyers. I have always been good at reading people and I have been a good judge of character, and there was certainly something off about her approach. There is little point explaining the catalogue of events in great detail as it is old history. Briefly, we had a meeting about my support that really did not go very well and involved her amongst many other things bringing a bear sized dog with her! It was certainly one of the most intimidating experiences I have ever had.

I immediately made an extensive complaint about her actions to the fund which was mostly upheld although little else was done as the Independent Living Fund seemed to make one blunder after another. The fundamental point here was that my mental health was now suffering badly and it was not going to get better overnight.

After a period where I had felt safe and stable, even if it had been on weak foundations, Helen has unwittingly unravelled my mental stability, causing me to feel deeply unsafe and stressed. This would manifest itself in terms of severe insomnia, deep depression and huge stress. I became fragile and vulnerable with no support from my family, difficulties with my support staff, and few friends at that time.

The short term solution to my insomnia was alcohol, the best freely available, if sometimes expensive, self-prescribing medicine available to anyone who wanted it. My favourite poisons were whiskey and coke, or gin and orange juice or any type of smoothie. I also had a love of cocktails as well as wine, although I disliked any type of beer with a passion. So, as the stress and insomnia meant that my drinking slowly increased each day and night because it was something that could knock me out so I could get some kind of sleep. My evening personal assistant would often find me metaphorically hanging off the ceiling like Spiderman in a stupor of alcoholic daze as I was stressed in a way like never before or since.

My issues with the fund rumbled on for 18 months as their chief executive refused to answer many of my concerns, even when they were asked by a Community Care solicitor who I recruited from the local Law Centre. The main issue was that now I was lacking confidence and feeling vulnerable, I lacked any trust in social workers and any idea that I would receive a proper assessment. It therefore took a lot of reassurances for me to get the courage to have an assessment, which in the end went well.

While this period unleashed the worst of my still to be properly diagnosed mental health issues, which took many further years to properly resolve. The period also saw me embark with determination and drive on finding out as much as I could about the Independent Living Fund and social care generally. I was going to beat the system by knowing more about the fund better that even people working for the fund knew. I was going to become the expert in social care like no other service user had been before.

The major slap in the face from Helen Tyers had been a wake-up call that had provided me with the motivation to rebuild myself stronger and with more confidence. This was the moment I saw the need to develop my foundations as a full adult to which to grow upon. I was never going to let anyone to allow to attack my personhood or intimidate me again and get away with it, at least not in terms of face to face contact.

This was not going to be easy nor something that should be achieved overnight, and there was going to be a big price to pay over the next couple of years spreading over the whole of my 30s in one way or another. One of the causalities of the matter was my relationship with Patrick. In October 2004, we went on holiday with his mother and two of his personal assistants which was a total disaster for a lot of reasons. My drinking was certainly out of control and had not helped the situation.

We decided to end our formal relationship while remaining friends during the holiday, however after the holiday his mother and staff were putting their two pennies worth in which certainly did not help matters. Patrick and I ending up arguing on a variety of issues until he refused to speak to me, which lasted for 6 years. This was probably a good thing as I was not in a good place and I needed time to sort myself out without having to worry about him or maintaining a relationship. It was sad and I was immensely grateful when we began talking again.

The stress of the fund also related to my relationship with my personal assistants as it was their wages ultimately being discussed. While social workers may only ever see assessments and personal assistance in of what I just need in terms of what I need to meet my outcomes, and they do not see the practical and emotional impact that reducing a package 'just a few hours' has. For my existing staff, it may make a big difference to whether they can afford to work for me or whether they have to find a new job.

Since as personal assistant and employer, our relationship with each other can be more emotionally connected than other types of working relationships because of the personal nature of the work, asking someone to leave or having someone leave because of no fault of either party but rather something out of their control, is indeed quite distressing.

It is not only the actuality of this happening that is stressful, but the simple possibility of something happening, which is the potential with any assessment I have with any of the funders. As my support is reviewed by each funder potentially every 1 or 2 years for the rest of my life, you can start to understand the level of stress I am constantly under.

So, when one assessment appears to go pear shaped when there is a huge possibility of my staffing situation completely changing as well as many aspects of my life, initially for the worse, is extremely worrying and stressful. I know that in the long term I will survive whatever is thrown at me and that not knowing the outcome of a decision made about myself, especially when I have little control over it, can be more worrying and stressing than dealing with the actual consequences when a difficult decision has been made.

One of the frustrations I have with how the whole assessment process is currently organised is there is no credit provided for how long you have already had support, so you are always being treated as a new user by professionals who often have far less experience than myself. This means it is like playing snakes and ladders as you never know from year to year if you are going to be seen as a positive user they wish to showcase or a difficult user who gets want they want because of their reputation.

Helen Tyers had opened a hole in the emotional fibre of my life before walking away, and leaving other people's failure to resolve my issues to widen that hole larger and larger. My 30s was spent sinking into the hole to fight many of my demons so that I would be able to climb out slowly and carefully I stronger and more powerful individual free from much of the baggage I had so far retained from my childhood and 20s.

If I was going to be the inspiring leader in impairment and disability issues, I had to still that extra mile to protect myself from the past and prepare myself for the future. Helen Tyers may had been the catalyst for a bad period in my field, she showed me that my foundations were weak and my cupboard were bare, enabling me to build up from a period of collapse.

But I never gave up and even during my darkest of days, I will still be making a positive and meaningful contribution to society, putting on a smile to the outside world who were never fully aware of the problems I was facing.

21 The young enterprising brit

I have always believed in a balance of karma and while a lot of very unusual things always seem to happen to me, positive or negative, it always seems to be balanced out at the same time. If I was going to have a problem, it would always be a problem like no one has had before. If someone would have that very subtle piece of good luck without it being anything too big, then it would be me.

In this context, it is important to highlight that while I was having all the problems with the Independent Living Fund and Helen Tyers, I was having a lot of success with my business and with one particular customer, Scope. I had been involved with Scope, a charity aimed at supporting people with cerebral palsy at that time, in a voluntary capacity since 1994 when they had changed their name from the Spastics Society, a name I had really hated as I found the term really offensive. In 2000, after a lot of internal politics, I had decided I had done more than my fair share of voluntary work and if Scope wanted me to work for them again, it would have to be paid!

And this is what happened as literally straight after my meeting with Helen Tyers, I had another meeting with some of Scope's senior staff at Birmingham Airport. The meeting came about because I had built up a good relationship with the current Chief Executive, Tony Manwaring, who saw my potential to support the organisation. I would be a part of a team with 2 senior staff and another consultant that would do a complete review of the workings of the charity. This was real work with real pay!

As a result of this amazing opportunity, I started a retainer contract with Scope that lasted 3 years in total. The work kept changing because Scope was always changing, and not always for the better. Fundamentally I had almost unlimited access to the organisation's inner workings and I knew as much about the organisation as anyone could. But sadly, I was seeing it slow and painful demise as the organisation still exists but further from their glory days than ever before.

The organisation had been set up by parents to support people with cerebral palsy but by 2004 it had become a solely professional led organisation with a huge identity crisis. Cerebral palsy has had its day of being fashionable in the 1950s and 1960s, and it was not sexy enough for the thirty somethings non-impaired people now running the organisation's marketing and other activities. So slowly I watched Scope slowly abandon people with cerebral palsy in preference to being pan-impairment, focusing on more fashionable impairments like autism. Scope asked me to write a 'rough guide on cerebral palsy' which I started before they terminated the project behind my back, ending my relationship with the organisation in late 2007 on bad terms, and I have so far not been able to get my foot back in the door.

My business activities were now definitely focused on impairment and disability issues. I had now a set of branded services that covered the vast range of services that were being promoted on my ever changing website. I will not go into great detail into the services I was offering then or indeed now because firstly, all that information is on my website, and secondly, this is a story about my life and not a catalogue of my products and services.

One component of my work which many people will not be aware of is what I call my database. I started my database in 1992 as a collection of many different organisations in the UK and Internationally on many issues, particularly issues relating to impairment and disability. It started as an Outlook address book before moving to being an Evernote notebook currently.

I have tried to collect many useful organisations like the governing bodies of every issue locally, nationally, within Europe and across the world. Wherever I see a useful organisation or any organisation on the web, I add it to my database as they could be my next customer or be a useful contact in any piece of work I am doing. I like to format each organisation's note to include as much of their online and social media contact addresses, which is a never ending and thankless task, but one I find therapeutic as I call it my 'knitting'.

The primarily use of my database is as a tool to help me find new opportunities for work. Right for day one of starting my business, I have never known who would be my next customer, how I would find them and what the work could involve. I have always seen the form of marketing I have needed to do as similar to being a sea turtle laying its 1000s of eggs in the sand of the beach knowing that only a few hatched turtles would make it to the sea.

By this I mean I have needed to contact as many potential customers as I could in any way I can from networking, cold emails and now using social media. Only a small proportion of these interactions would end up generating leads, and only a few leads will end up being turned into actual paid work. And because a lot of my work is very unique and ad-hoc, meeting the needs of specific customers at specific times for specific reasons, it does not often lead to repeat work. This means marketing has become an endless activity which I keep improving as the one activity I mostly spend my time going.

After bobbing alone for a few years, I needed some level of recognition to boast my position and in November 2004, this would come unexpectedly from a national campaign that was going deliver exactly what I needed. In that summer, I received an email from someone from Young Enterprise asking me if I minded if they entered me for a competition called Enterprising Young Brits. I replied of course and left it at that, hearing nothing about it until months after.

Then in the October, I received a letter from Enterprise Week to say I have been selected to be a finalist in the Community category of Enterprising Young Brits as well as inviting me and a guest to come to the final at a top London hotel the night before, stay over, and present to a panel in the morning so they could decide the winners, to be announced in the afternoon with awards presented by Gordon Brown, who was the Chancellor of the Exchequer at that time. I must had read the letter 50 times with glee.

The first thing to understand here is that this was a mainstream competition that had nothing to do with dysability, so being a finalist meant my enterprising skills were being measured compared to everyone else regarding of my impairment. I spent a lot of time preparing my presentation for the panel, making it as perfect as I could. The night before the final at the hotel I was extremely nervous and I am not sure I slept much.

While the other finalists in all the hotel the night before, we did not properly meet each other until the morning of the presentations on 15th November 2004. As usual in these situations, I was the only finalist with any kind of obvious impairment. When it was time for my presentation, I think I wowed them, despite having a speech impairment, I had now learnt how to present myself in a way that was better than most. After I had presented I went for a brief walk to get some fresh air with my personal assistant of the time, where I told her if this world was fair than I really deserved to win this.

After a networking lunch where we are all very nervous, we waited for Gordon Brown to come. Then the winners of each category were announced. When it came to my category and I was announced as the winner I yelped for joy, making half the people in the room jump as I was now heading up to the stage to collect my award. There is a great picture of me walking up to the stage that shows great pride and determination. I am certainly convinced Gordon Brown had not been expecting me with my helmet at an event like this.

The award was a catalyst for a whole range of local and national media interviews including the Daily Mail, Metro and others. As I was now a part of a small elite of Enterprise Ambassadors that grew as the competition was repeated for several years, I received many invites to networking events including one at Number 11, Downing Street! It may not have directly got me more leads or work, but it certainly helped my image and reputation at that time.

The award was very special to me because it demonstrated people were recognising my talents as a person regardless of my impairment. As someone with a speech impairment, who drools and uses a helmet, I had started to break through the stereotypes of what someone like myself could do and become. I had still a long way to go, but I was now somewhere on the hard and long road towards success.

22 Suicidal wishes

As I have discussed previously, my thirties were full of ups and downs, often at the same time. While my work was going well, and I could put on a brave face to the outside world, at home, things had taken a turn for the worse as I continued to sink deeper into a state of despair that did not show any sign of improving.

By 2006, two years after Helen Tyers had started a process that slowly unrivalled my life, I remained in a period of deep depression. I was still drinking a lot most of the day as a form of chemical and emotionally. My financial situation has become more unstable as I had run up a lot of credit card debts which is a story for another time. While I had a good personal assistant from Zimbabwe in the weekdays, my weekend cover had lurched from one disaster to the next, causing my mental wellbeing to weaken further. While my work from Scope was going well, everything else seemed to be going pear shaped. I was also only sleeping a few hours at one time.

In May 2006, there was a fateful weekend when everything seemed to come to a head. If we can firstly understand that I was already at one of my lowest points anyway, and that all the events of the weekend were on top of this. On the Friday night, there was a huge and close thunderstorm. I suddenly heard an extremely loud clap of thunder which must have hit something very close because it knocked out my Sky TV box as well as the modem on my computer.

Now as someone living on my own with very little weekend personal assistant cover, the TV and the internet were vital to what was left of my sanity. I had started to use Secondlife, which I will explain in another chapter, and my explorations that weekend what not going that well. I had hit rock bottom and I was feeling suicidal. In a mad panic of ultimate frustration, I wrapped the cord of my home telephone around my neck is a stupid attempt to end it all.

When I am myself, I very much oppose suicide as a solution, since it is a short-term and everlasting solution to what is often a very complex problem that often and mostly relates to people's environment. The feeling of suicide is real and I believe stems from an immediate inability to see other options or ways to solve the problems we are currently facing.

For myself, I was extremely emotionally tired as I just did not see an end to the endless problems I was facing. I knew I had already made a huge contribution to society in many ways, certainly more than most people. I felt I had already earned enough points many times over to get into heaven or whatever the afterlife was going to be, and that anything I did now was just a bonus. I was tired and perhaps this was my time to go?

While I respected other people's religious beliefs, so long as they did not thrust them down my throat, I did not belong to any religion myself. If I believed in God, it would be as someone with many flaws who I would very much like to have a word with as there was many things I wanted to set him straight on. If and when my life became complex, I would joke that God was playing games with me for his perverted amusement.

I do believe in destiny and my faith is in myself and everyone else, as I regard everyone regardless of their background to have the potential to make a meaningful contribution to society. As I will explain more in another chapter, this belief system has made me very unpopular with other 'disabled' activists and campaigners.

I believe in destiny as a coping mechanism to understand why my life feels so complex and unique. Yes, I know we are all unique and special, and I am certainly not the most important person in the world as we are all equal, but particularly for someone with my level of impairment, I had done things few people have. My journey is unique and interesting because of the wide range of people I have impacted in large and small ways over the years.

But my uniqueness had a price and I appeared to be now paying for it. If I had known my many further achievements to come, I would had kept going for sure, but for now, I was ready to end my life as I remained in deep depression.

On the Saturday on the weekend, a friend helped me sort out my modem so at least I had the internet. I know I needed help with my mental health and so I rung the crisis team, who came and they were utterly useless as their advice was simply stop drinking, with no willingness to understand my full situation.

On the Sunday, I told a former young personal assistant about how I was feeling and her father arranged for the police to escort me to hospital for a mental health assessment. Again, this was utterly useless as they simply said I needed a holiday, which is not as stress-free as it should be when you have a significant impairment. However, the patronising and arrogant way I was treated by the assessors did put some fire in my belly as I refused to be ignored in this way.

I think this may have been the moment my situation changed direction as I realised it was time for me to take the bull by the horns and sort my life out. This was reinforced for me when I unexpectedly received an invite to the Snowdon's Trust 25th Anniversary reception with Cherie Blair at Number 10, Downing Street.

The Snowdon Trust was a charity set up by Lord Snowdon to support people with impairments with taking part in Higher Education, providing individuals grants to assist them with meeting any extra costs they may have. Before this point, I vaguely knew about the charity although I had never had any dealings with them. I was therefore pleasantly surprised to get the invite.

The event itself had just what the doctor had order, something exciting, rewarding and interesting. I was highly impressed at how the Downing Street staff serving the canapés discreetly feeding me them directly into my mouth like it was an everyday occurrence. I was also impressed and inspired by the fact I had been inviting the event simply because of the information on my website about my work and because I was the right fit.

It became to restore my faith in myself and demonstrate I still had a lot to offer the world. I was inspiring others in a way that technology was allowing, which would have been impossible just a decade or so before. This gave me further motivation to get back to restoring my life. It was going to be a long process with a lot of unexpected hurdles along the way but it was something I had to do and I deserved to achieve.

I believe you can not have any meaningful appreciation for the good life if you have not experienced hardship in one way or another. My voyage into the realms of suicide as provided me with a better understanding of my own experience and the experience of others.

My brief desire to commit suicide was a rational decision based on the information I had at that time, even if it was the wrong decision to make. I believe unless someone is in the final stages of dying, where the focus is about having a good death, as oppose as a painful one, life is far too precious to waste. I do not care how severely impaired someone may be or may become, if they can make someone else smile then they have important value to all of us. I am pro-choice when it comes to abortion as people's situations can be complex, but I hope for a society and political environment when a positive attitude towards impairment means that this is not a deciding factor in the way it is now.

My self-worth plays an important factor in my mental well being. I need to be able to contribute to others and be recognised as someone who is able to contribute to others, During my 30s, I would do a lot of thinking about my place in society as my role and purpose became clearly, as well as the further development of my unique viewpoints that would put me at odds with mainstream thinking on many issues.

My mental wellbeing was something I was starting to understand better and realise that it would be something I would need to keep working on to find a state of stability and happiness.

23 A mugging of change

I moved from Sadler Road to Treforest Road in 1999. The reason for this was that it was an upgrade from one bedroom to two. The local council was promoting its properties in their less desirable areas, and offering single people like myself two bedroom properties, long before the idea of the bedroom tax ever existed.

Treforest Road was on the Stoke Aldermoor housing estate, which was not the roughest part of Coventry but it had its reputation. I was well aware of the area's reputation before I moved there but I felt and still feel it was a good opportunity to have a larger place that suited my needs at that time.

For the most part, I had a very good time at Treforest Road although there were a number of incidents that were problematic of the area I was living in. While I attempted to keep myself to myself, it is very difficult not to be noticed around the estate when you have a significant impairment.

The incidents included having my laptop stolen when I was in London one evening, having a brick through my window and having a brick through of the car of a friend who was visiting me. I never felt intimidated by what was happening and I had no hesitation to contact the police immediately after every incident even if that did not result in much action. There was one point where I had a police camera in my home to monitor any criminal behaviour towards me.

While we live in an era of increased awareness of hate crime towards people with impairments, I never felt and still do not feel that these incidents were related to any notion of hatred towards me. I had chosen to live in this area where they were a lot of young people who have brought up to accept anti-social behaviour, a fact of the welfare state many dinner table activists currently refuse to believe exist.

I was just an easy and vulnerable person to pick up when the opportunity arose, even if I did not feel vulnerable. I must had been known around the estate as the disabled guy but I certainly did not feel it was personal. In fact, I built up a sense that within the code of honour that probably existed around the estate's anti-social community, that picking on significantly impaired people like myself was not the done thing. I can only imagine that those foolish enough to break the code were punished in one way or another.

Things changed in the summer of 2006. It was a very hot summer and despite living on the ground floor, I had my windows open in the day and at night because of the heat. If you remember that I was still not sleeping very well and I was spending a lot of the night awake using my computer. I had really got into Secondlife, which I will explain properly in another chapter, and I was now spending most of my nights in a virtual nightclub called The Blarney Stone in a virtual sim called Dublin. I know it is hard to imagine if you have no understanding of Secondlife, but I was basically dancing the night away each night.

So I could really enjoy the music without disturbing my neighbours in the middle of the night, I had headphones on. If you also understand as I was living on my own and it was hot, I was not wearing any clothes, you can start to imagine my situation. So basically, I was mugged in my own home twice in the middle of the night.

The first time someone knocked on my front door pretending to be the son of one of my formal personal assistants while someone else jumped into my home via the bedroom window. The second time, they just jumped in my bedroom window while I was on my computer with my headphones on completely naked. I remember fighting back that last once and maybe both times. What occurred happened very quickly and it is difficult looking back to remember the events in full. I also unsure if they took much, if anything.

I would be lying if I did not say these muggings did not shake me up although I was annoyed and determined as opposed to anything else. Treforest Road had served me well but it was now time to move on. I was tired of the anti-social behaviour I had been experiencing and it was time to find somewhere in a safer area. The second mugging was also a catalyst for me to say it was now really time for me to put my life back on track from the backwards spiral I had been experiencing since Helen Tyers. I needed to stop feeling sorry for myself and start rebuilding my life up again brick by brick.

If I was going to have to move, then I was going to make it worthwhile. I had been pondering the idea of having a live-in volunteer for some time now but in order to do that and indeed, before I could even consider doing that, I needed another (third) bedroom, since I was using my second bedroom as an office. This was again still an era before the bedroom tax when having a third would simply be an advantage.

I also controversially decided that at this time in my life I wanted to live on the first floor, even if there was no lift, as oppose to the ground floor. I wanted to feel safe and be able to open my windows at night without the risk of being mugged, etc. I did not have an obsessional fear but I was coming out of a very vulnerable stage of my life and I needed security and stability. I was still able to mostly walk indoors and outdoors, and if there was ever going to be a time when I could not manage the stairs, I would find a way around it.

With a clearly picture of what I wanted I wrote to the housing association which had now taken over the property from the local council with my concerns about my situation and the precise type of accommodation I was looking for. It seemed to me that a lot of money had been pumped into Stoke Aldermoor because of the level of anti-social behaviour occurring, which was clearly benefiting the housing association and local council, as well as the police. I therefore had a suspicion that my crimes I had experienced had not been investigated as thoroughly as they could have been because there was a financial interest by the many organisations to keep the crime rate in the area to a higher than usual level.

I put my suspicions and concerns in my letter, suggesting that if the housing association would not find suitable accommodation for me to move from the estate, they would seriously need to look at how they can improve my security and safety on the estate. While I never got any response about my suspicions either confirming or denying them, I did get precisely the type of accommodation I was looking for in a relatively short amount of time.

Everdon Road in the Holbrooks area of Coventry as exactly what I had been looking for. It was a three bedroom place on the first floor. It had no lift but the stairs were easily manageable at that time for me. After a few years of hell stemming from the actions of Helen Tyers, this was going to be the start of a fresh start.

I never regretted living at Treforest Road, and I certainly did not feel scarred by the anti-social experiences I had. It clearly made me more aware of the need to feel and actually be safe, and that the active safeguarding of myself was an activity that could never be forgotten.

I was also learning that everything in life has a beginning, middle and end, and that their own story was often unpredictable. Treforest Road had been exactly what I needed when I needed it, but it will now time to move onto a new chapter in my life with a different series of ups and downs. I was now determined to rebuild my life after such a difficult patch.

24 New home new chances

Moving to Everdon Road was a chance to rebuild my life but it was going to be a long road to not only restore what I had previously but to become a better person. I still had a lot of issues to resolved. While my mental health was improving, I will still highly dependent on alcohol for physical as well as emotional reasons.

The move to Everdon Road coincided with a change in my main personal assistant as I recruited Flora. Flora used to work for me when I had staff from a care agency and we had kept in contact through the years. She had emailed me just before I moved asking about work and I jumped at the chance of having her as a part of my team. She began working for me at the weekends before going full-time with me in October 2007.

Another big issue for me to sort out was my financial situation. Since leaving university I had managed to acquire many credit cards and I had managed to acquire a lot of debt, we are talking over £50000. I believe as well as the practical reasons of buying stuff I probably did not always need, there were a number of psychological reasons for this.

I believe the first of these was because my mother used to be very strict about money due to her own psychological reasons. She used to severely berate me if I was perceived to waste even a penny on anything she regarded as unnecessary. This meant as soon as I began to have my own spending power away from her influence I made the most of it. I did learn to be wise with money but I also did rebel against her restrictions. I wanted to enjoy the moment, celebrating the achievements I have made in my freedom as someone with a significant impairment who was able to make his own mistakes free from anyone else.

I believe a second reason was my still undiagnosed mental health issues that were akin to mild bipolar. As a part of my condition I had short cycles of depression and mania, to the point where I could have both traits at the same time. Feeling safe, secure and happy used to involve spending a lot of money, especially when I lacked the foundations I have now. It was and probably remained an addiction that is as hard to stop as any other addiction. People talk about retail therapy as some kind of joke but for myself, it was really a form of therapy and one I still use.

By 2007, I had got my spending under control because it was a case of having to. This meant that it was time to sort out my debts once in for all. I believe in 2005 I had started exploring an Individual Voluntary Arrangement with Grant Thomson. This was not bankruptcy but rather a three year deal to pay my creditors an amount I could afford each month during this period and then the rest would be wiped off and I would then be debt free. This was quite a complex process with a lot of rules and regulations.

At the start this was working well but during my great depression of 2006, I started to miss payments. When I hit rock bottom, my priorities became irrational and the process of depression with an excessive use of alcohol was a costly business added to the fact my income had reduced as my work was suffering.

So, in 2007, the arrangement had collapsed and the next stage as stated in the arrangement was for Grant Thomson to petition the courts to make me bankrupt. I should say right now that I probably know that bankruptcy was the only option left available for me but I was not going to go down without a fight. I had not liked how Grant Thomson had been treating me and I was not going to make it easy for them.

What is supposed to happen when you go bankrupt is that the petitioner, Grant Thomson, presents their case in person to the judge and if I choose to be present, my role is to bow my head, say I agree with the petitioner and the matter is over and done with within 5 minutes. This was certainly not what happened with my bankruptcy court case.

I had learnt a while ago that the best way to deal with these kind of situations is to tell the truth, the whole truth and lots of it! While it is important to keep focused, it can be helpful to explain the background to a situation in as much detail as possible so people can better understand where I am coming from. This is especially important for myself as my situation is often so very different to other people's. So my submission to response to the petitioner's case ran into many pages as I put my heart and soul on the line.

So what was supposed to be a simple 5 minute case ending up taking several hearings spread across several months. The conclusion was obvious, that I was declared bankrupt in February 2008. But I was glad that I tried to defend myself for sanity as opposed to anything else, and it helped me to accept the decision. Since I had been representing myself, it had not costed me a penny as Flora was translating for me during the hearings.

Now I had been declared bankrupt, the next stage was to meet with the Insolvency Service to process my bankruptcy. Since I had no assets of real value, despite my large collection of overalls, swimming hats and wetsuits, this was really a very simple process. I think the case officer was somehow out of his depth and it was not every day that he had to deal with someone with a significant level of cerebral palsy.

Since I had no real assets and for once there were no other real complications, I was only declared bankrupt for just 12 months. This meant I could not be a director of any commercial or charitable organisation, so this also meant Enable Enterprises had to wound up as I became self-employed in the way I am currently straight after I was declared bankrupt.

I also had to open a basic bank account and slowly work myself up to having many of the features I rely upon now like online banking, and a contactless direct card. Financially, after the bankruptcy, while there was a very brief threat from the case officer about his capacity to take my computer away from me, I could keep all the tools of my trade. If he had taken my computer, which is fundamental to my very existence, I imagined myself laying down in front of his car before he could drive off with it. I would have certainly caused a huge stink that would had been very difficult to ignore.

Bankruptcy was much easier than I had imagined it would be, and I was glad that in the end it happened. I was also pleased that I had experienced something many entrepreneurs go though as a part of their own learning experience. Unlike so many people with impairments, especially people with significant or severe impairments, I had the real freedom to make mistakes, large and small, and learn from them in the same way as anyone else.

I did not miss the fact my company was gone as I know as the opportunity to carve myself as an Independent Disability Consultant. It did not change what I did on a day to day basis, as I continued to carry on finding work in my usual fashion. I chose to add the term Independent to my job title at this stage to show that I was independent from any other organisations as well as being independent in my thinking. This has been very important in rebuilding my image as my fame and influence grew, and I would find myself increasingly at odds with other activists and campaigners in my fields of work.

With my financial situation sorted for the time being at least, I was still working and looking for that piece of work, my golden egg, that would provide me with financial stability once and for all, something I am still looking for as I write my story currently. While my work has always been ad-hoc, with ups and downs, I have never given up the idea that I would reach a period of financial stability.

But it was now time to focus on other issues like my health, which was still in a dreadful state. I was also still building a home for myself at Everdon Road with foundations and roots. I vowed I was going to remain safe and secure to a level never reached before this point.

Living in Everdon Road was a change and a fresh start with many new and wonderful opportunities I did not believe were possible previously. My struggles were very far from over and I still had a lot of learning to get completely where I wanted to go as my 30s still remained years of hard work and struggle, but I was still moving forward in building an adult version of myself with the same values and beliefs that I have always had along with a new sense of confidence, experience, expertise and maturity without ever losing my imagination and sense of humour, and mischief.

25 A second life

It is sometimes the smallest things in life that can make the biggest difference to yourself, to others around you, and to the whole world in general. Secondlife and Wheelies were examples of what happens when this is taken to the extreme as it remains one of the most interesting and fascinating achievements of my life.

Secondlife can be best described as a virtual world that during its peak, had over ten million users or residents. The residents are portrayed as avatars and it is possible to customise their appearance in an infinite number of ways into being something that adequately represents your real self or to be something very different. It is the residents themselves that build their own environments on land they have purchased and pay fees on to the owners of Secondlife, Linden Labs.

From the comfort of your own home and computer, you can do anything you can do in real life in Secondlife, from dancing to flying yourself as well as aircraft, to fighting dragons, playing any kind of sport, attending lectures, playing board games and the list goes on and on. It is however very important to understand that Secondlife is a virtual environment that can be used for leisure, education or business and it is not a game. For many of its residents, it is a serious platform that has often resulted in life changing consequences, including for myself.

My secondlife story has been well documented in other places but here is an overview and reflection over a decade later. I first entered Secondlife on 4th May 2006 after I had received an email newsletter from a colleague that briefly mentioned the platform.

I do not remember the specifics but on my first day someone provided me with a wheelchair, and a few weeks later someone made me a helmet in the style I used in real life. My decision to use a wheelchair was a natural one and one I never give any second thought. Since I had a visible significant impairment in real life, I wanted to replicate them in Secondlife so I did not have to keep explaining my impairment to people, since it was a core part of my identity.

I had no idea that my use of a wheelchair would be considered so ground-breaking across the real world. At the time I started using Secondlife, it was seen as a virtual utopia where people with impairments and many others could escape their real lives and be free to take on escapist activities. The idea that someone would want to bring their impairment into Secondlife was revolutionary and caused a lot of excitement within the media and academic fields across the real world.

Secondlife was full of nightclubs and as a budding entrepreneur, I wanted my own nightclub. Having a club involved having land, building a club environment, hiring DJs and live artists as well as a manager to manage them, and finally having guests to dance the night away. I put all this in place with the ambition of being the best and most friendly club in Secondlife. While the club had always been for everyone and it was never specifically designed for people with impairments or wheelchair users, I decided to tongue-in-cheek give the club a disability-theme and so I called it Wheelies.

The launch of Wheelies at 9pm UK time on 1st September 2006 went extremely well and it quickly grew into a great club. Over the ten years it existed it had a very complex history of ups and downs with many dramas, many rebuilds, many managers, many fun nights and many happy guests. It quickly became widely known in Secondlife for a comfortable and safe place for people with impairments whether they wished to make their impairments visible or not, as well as for anyone else free of prejudice whatever kind the representation they used.

As well as being widely known within Secondlife and its internal media, which I would have expected, I however did not expect the club or myself to develop so much attention from the mainstream media. Secondlife was growing and so it was receiving a lot of media interest, and Wheelies was a great human interest story that the media often latched onto. The first big media story was in October 2006, when I was interview for a piece Canada's CBC News did on Secondlife, which included a comprehensive feature of Wheelies and myself.

This started an avalanche of media interest that is too numerous to completely list but included Newsweek International, CNN website, The Times and BBC World service. Wheelies was just a small idea I was mostly funding out of my own pocket designed for a minority interest on a minority platform, so this attention was crazy. There was a time where every few days I was receiving a media request or some academic students was asking me questions about Wheelies or myself. Google is now full of references about the club.

The irony was I applied and was successful is being a contestant in Secondlife's official version of Big Brother. Big Brother was something I always went to do and it is still something I often dream about, in terms of the television version. The fact you would unlikely to have known about me being on Big Brother until this moment shows that the 'show' was a media flop and certainly did not help me as Wheelies received far more publicity in the short term and the long term.

The biggest achievement for the club and myself in terms of Secondlife was when Wheelies won the Revolutionary Award of the Catalysts Award in 2008. This was a competition for technology based start-up companies and others very similar to Enterprising Young Brits. The award was once again presented by Gordon Brown, who was now Prime Minister at that time. It was amazing what was just a bit of fun that made such a big impact to myself and so many other people around the world in a manner beyond my imagination.

One of the biggest real life activities I did because of Secondlife was attend the Secondlife Community Convention (SLCC) in Chicago in 2007, where I did a presentation about Wheelies and my experiences of Secondlife. I flew from Birmingham to Boston, where I met a friend I met on Internet Relay Chat before the days of Facebook who had followed my interest in Secondlife, Rick. Rick was an amazing friend who had a great understanding of impairment issues although we had never met in person before this time. He was going to assist me in what remains an adventure of a lifetime.

From Boston we caught the Amtrak train to Washington DC, going First Class. We did not have a lot of time in Washington before we had to catch our next overnight train in a disabled sleeper carriage, so I decided we would jump in a taxi and go around the Whitehouse, which we saw, and go straight back to the train station. The train to Chicago was about 12 hours and it was an exciting journey. It was experiences like this that made me feel alive and that I am going something beyond what was ever expected of me, even if I was not the first person with a significant impairment to have some of these experiences.

The convention was amazing as it was an opportunity to meet a lot of people I knew well in Secondlife but I have never met in person and maybe unlikely to ever meet in person again. As usual, despite it being a big convention, I was the only one with a significant impairment and it was great to be a part of this community in Secondlife as well as now in real life. I also had the opportunity to meet up with some of the other people involved with Wheelies. It was a great time.

As you may have gathered, while Secondlife still has an active community, it never made it into the mainstream like Facebook or Twitter. I think one reason for this is that it remains intense both in terms of the CPU processing the software requires and the concentration and focus required in be in-world, in the same way 3D television failed.

While I enjoyed Wheelies and it was amazing in its glory days, it was expensive to run and I could not afford to continue to run it after the media attention had died down and the platform has gone stale for me as other technology and issues took priority. I recently retired once and for all from the club and my understanding is that the club has now vanished into the mists of time.

I have many good memories from Wheelies and it played a very important role in my mental wellbeing, especially when I was feeling down. The club's theme song was Proud by Heather Small, which is my favourite song and has become my own theme song. I am very proud of Wheelies and everything it achieved in its history.

26 He lives with me

One of the main reasons for having an extra bedroom at Everdon Road was because I was interested in having live-in volunteers from an organisation previously called Community Service Volunteers (CSV), now called Volunteer Matters. The volunteers would work for me for up to 12 months 35 hours per week, working in the evenings and weekends, living with myself, and they would receive an expenses and food allowance. As well as having their own room, they would have access to all the main facilities of my own home like my kitchen and bathroom, leaving me with the privacy of my bedroom and office. I was only looking for male volunteers as I could not imagine living with a woman as I think it would become uncomfortable.

CSV were taking an incredibly long time to set up the project in terms of all the paperwork and I particularly remember being stuck for several months on the health and safety statement, and so I decided that I would have a try at doing it myself, independently from any organisation. I had become real life friends with a fellow contestant from the Secondlife's version of Big Brother called Fabian, and I offered him the opportunity to live and work with me.

Fabian ended up being an odd person indeed which included the fact he wanted to be a she because he thought women had an easier life! After a few weeks of him working for me it was very clear that he was not cut out for working as a personal assistant and while I had sacked him, he refused to leave my property because he was insistent that he could get social housing in Coventry, despite being single and living in Watford a in safe environment with his mother. One weekend I demanded he left or there would be consequences and there were as on the Sunday morning I contacted his mother to come and collect him as he finally got the message. The next stage would have been to call the police and have him forcibly removed as I was never someone to mess about with.

So, it was time to give CSV a second chance and this time the project finally got off the ground with Flora being the supervisor for the volunteers. This meant that it was her role, as well as being my main personal assistant, to assist me with the induction of the volunteers and to be a someone the volunteers could go to if they had a problem or issue they felt unable to discuss with myself. While it would very rarely be needed, it was also Flora's role to mediate between the volunteer and myself if there was a major conflict. I trusted Flora because she was always honest and told me when she disagreed with me.

My first set of volunteers were mostly from Germany, 5 of them, with one guy from France, Wael, who did not work out very well for various reasons. At the start of the project, all German males had to do a year in the Army as a part of their national service, or they could choose to do some kind of civil service and this is where 'volunteering' for me came in. The German government however abandoned the idea in 2012

My first volunteer was Stefan, who started in September 2008. I was firstly surprised at how accepting I was mostly to living with someone else after living on my own for 16 years. There was however still a lot of learning to be done as I got used to this new kind of support. With the help of Stefan and Flora, I produced a code of conduct for the future volunteers that became a working document that evolved through the years.

I really liked what the volunteers did for me as it contrasted well with Flora's role. Flora's work was about providing me stability and assisting me with managing my home and work life. The volunteer's role was to assist me with my leisure activities and my travelling exploits. While going away with me overnight or longer was an exciting opportunity for the volunteer, it was a hassle for Flora as it would be time away from her family. It would also be a good way to get the support from younger men in a manner that would unlikely work in a normal personal assistant relationship.

While I began to build up a bigger on people's culture according to the country the volunteers were from, I also knew they were individuals and I had a different relationship with each one of them. As I write this I have had volunteers from Germany, France, UK and my last few had been from Columbia, which is set to continue. Based on what I had learnt about their cultures, I created as saying that went; the British think they are right, the Germans know they are right, the French are just right, and the Columbians don't really care so long as they are happy.

The project has a whole went extremely well and so far there has not been any major disasters. As young men using this time aboard to develop themselves and their personhood, I have always expected them to have weaknesses and flaws which I would always work about. Because I had Flora and I knew by now from bitter experience how to keep myself safe when I was depending on those who remained at times complete strangers, I never allowed myself to become over reliant on the volunteers.

Two of the projects has ended early for reasons related to what the volunteers where they were on their emotional journeys, which was fair enough, and neither of the projects ended in what I would consider as a disaster. My less favourite volunteer was a German called Kristof who was an absolute bully both to myself and Flora. He had very sexist views towards women that both Flora and myself found unacceptable. He thought his place in society made him better than anyone else, despite the fact he was supposedly supporting me for a year. I have a way of subtly dealing with people like him and by the end of the project, he understood that I had caught him out and I could not be intimidated in the long term.

My oddest volunteer was another German called Lars. Lars basically spent the whole of the project in his room, like he had metaphorically never left Germany. Whenever Flora or myself asked him a question, even at the end of the project, he responded with shock like a rabbit who has been caught in the headlights of a car. He kept receiving huge boxes from his mother, which was fine until I realised he had little intention to pack up his stuff when it was time for him to leave the project. He finally left the project with simply a lighted filled rucksack while leaving a huge box of his belongings in what was his room assuming his mother would arrange for someone to pick it up, which sent me slightly crazy in frustration.

Having live-in volunteers has probably remained when of the best decisions I have made, as well as recruiting Flora. Together, it has provided a level of stability in my personal support I have not experienced previously, allowing be to move forward with my life in terms of my home, leisure and work.

While the volunteers have never worked for officially overnight, it was always nice to know that I had some around in case I had an emergency like a nearby fire, a police issue or if I had suddenly become unwell. I however never insisted they stayed at home with me if they were not working as I always want them to help them most of the other activities the project offered outside work like the opportunity to travel around the country as well as internationally.

I also wanted to be as relaxed as I could with my volunteers in terms of house roles, providing them with a level of freedom that they may not have living with their parents. So long as I got what I needed and wanted, I was always happy for them to have as much freedom as they could. While it is their role to support me with my journey and my story, it was the role of Flora and myself to support them with their journey during the time they were living with me. It was an interdependency that I really liked since I was giving as well as taking.

Going forward, I hope to have many more live-in volunteers for however long I find the scheme suitable to my needs and aspirations. It has served me well so far and provided me with a security and foundation I really appreciate and enjoy as an important influence in my life.

27 A drink too far

Alcohol has always paid a role in my adult life, sometimes in a positive way and sometimes in a negative one. I have never smoked, I took or rather tried to take one puff of my 19th birthday, felt this soggy texture on my lips and thought, what is the point?! I have also never taken any form of recreational drugs as I always felt if you were always a worrier like myself than you would more likely to end up with a bad trip which would not be a nice experience. I have never liked passive smoking although I have never been highly moralistic about any kind of vice, legal or otherwise.

Before I was 18, my favourite tipple was Baileys and I always had a very sweet tooth when it came to alcohol. At the party when I was a 17 I had a few vodka and oranges, which kind of freaked my step-father out as he was unsure how the alcohol would react with me despite the fact I was not even on any medication at the time, and it was actually an odd over-reaction. Alcohol relaxed my muscles and my mind in the same way as everyone else.

When I went to university it was an opportunity to really experment with my tastes with the freedom of being in control of my own destiny. As I said previously, I quickly established that I did not like beer of any kind and that I could not stand the stuff. I also discovered that practically anything else was drinkable for me and I particularly liked creamy liqueurs and any kind of cocktails, especially the sweet tasting ones.

It was when I was doing the European Human Bridges projects that taste for the harder stuff began. Many of the leaders from other European countries would bring home made 100% proof spirits with them, where you needed to be rather drunk to be able to even attempt to drink them! Our seminars were full of very heavy late night drinking sessions. These were some of the most enjoyable nights of my life because these were the sessions where I made some of my closest friendships with people across Europe that have lasted a lifetime, even it is not often we are in contact or meet in person.

I would like to suggest that during my 20s, that my use of alcohol was pretty average and that it was merely for recreational usage as well as generally relaxing in the evenings. My usage may have been heavier than the average person but I did not think it was anything to worry about. It was in my 30s that my usage started to raise from a minor concern to a major concern.

As I have said previously, the stressed initiated by Helen Tyers, caused me to turn to alcohol for solutions. As someone with a naturally overactive mind I would worry about things at great speed, making it difficult for me to do anything else, and especially to calm down. I therefore used alcohol to slow down my mind to the point that I was able to sleep. It may have not been the best sleep or even a good sleep, but it was better than no sleep at all. I also found alcohol to be a great muscle relaxant, especially when I had a knotted or tight stomach that would make me feel nervous. I knew using alcohol in this way was not good but I did not have alternative solutions.

I did ask for help for many professional organisation about my alcohol usage and my general mental wellbeing on many occasions with little success. As I had said a few times so far, my mental health issues, which I probably had throughout my life, had not been diagnosed, properly or otherwise, and therefore I could not duly understand my situation, let alone know how it could be managed through treatments and therapies.

I had got through and I was going through a lot on many levels, without the support of my family and only with the full understanding of a handful of people. The physiological and sociological pressures that had been placed on myself would had broken anyone and for me, I was not surprised that I had found alcohol as a poorly designed solution to relieve the pressures I felt under. Maybe this was my excuse but who said I had to be perfect? In order to have achieved what I had achieved with the societal oppression I had faced since birth as someone with a significant impairment, there had to be some cracks in my armoury.

From the spring of 2004 until January 2009, almost five years, my drinking had become something systematic as I was drinking about a litre of gin a day with juices. To the outside world, I was functioning as well as anyone could. While I had always had my moments of frustration whether I had a drink or not, especially in terms of arguing with people online, the constant and deliberate use of alcohol kept me functional and away from withdrawal symptoms. I was never drunk in my appearance or behaviour, and my ability to write articles and perform work was never overly impaired.

But after five years of constant and heavy alcohol usage was clearly going to significantly impact on my health. As I mentioned previously, this was firstly in terms of my quality of sleep and sleeping patterns. For a long time I could not sleep more than 2 hours sleep at one time before waking up and needing a drink. This meant I would sleep at odd times during the day and night, working as much as I could whenever I was awake at what time that was.

It was certainly not a good time for me in terms of my sleep. I knew I was in a rut and I know I had to do something before something gave in, but even towards 2008, I still did not feel strong enough to do anything properly about it. This was my choice and only I could change the issue when I was ready to do so, and I know there would be a time when I would simply stop drinking.

My excessive use of alcohol was also seriously affecting my teeth, or rather the excessive use of fruit juice I was drinking with the alcohol. Within a year or so around 2008, my teeth had decayed to a such a significant amount that my regular dentist had to refer me to the top NHS Dentist in the city. My teeth were now in a constant state of infection and many of my teeth had sharp edges so I was continuously cutting my tongue, lips and sides of my mouth, especially since many of the movements in my mouth are uncontrollable due to my cerebral palsy.

The dentist tried his best to try to resolve the issue a bit at a time, appointment by appointment, but the work needed was too substantial, especially since the decay was still continuing. It required a more radical solution, which is why together we came up with the idea of removing all my teeth apart from my two front teeth, which could be built up to frame my appearance. This would require a full operation in hospital under general anaesthetic.

And so in January 2009, this is exactly what happened and the operation went extremely well. While I started with softer foods during the recovery period, it was long not before I was eating everything I was eating previously using my gums, which had now hardened accordingly. I have not considered and did not want dentures as I was managing very well without them, and with my cerebral palsy, I could not imagine myself keeping them in properly as I believed they may end up being more hassle than they were worth.

In January 2009, the alcohol usage stopped for the time being and although I had not realised it at that time, I had not escaped without some permanent life changing damage that would make 2009 one of the difficult periods of my life as the next chapter will tell. Despite this, I do not regret my alcohol usage throughout my adulthood and it is what it is, and there were certainly times when my alcohol usage kept my sane and alive, probably avoiding any real attempt of suicide.

I also generally have no regrets in my life because how can you learn if you are unable to make any mistakes? And I believe that if you were able to go back in time and change one small mistake you have made, it may have serious repercussions for many other situations that mean you will just make other mistakes. I prefer to believe for my own sanity that while we have free choice, everything has happened for a reason, a positive one in the long term, we are yet to understand, and therefore there is little point about stressing about what has happened.

28 A nervous time

The events I experienced in the first half of 2009 have been well documented in a publication called Llamdos Report and so this chapter is certainly not going to go into as much detail as this. It is however important to say that they were the most dramatic and disturbing collection of events I ever experienced that in the end would significantly push my life forward.

In 2008, I began to notice that my physical mobility appeared to be worsening. I felt that I could not walk as far as I used to which I simply put down to the fact I was getting older and my body was going to wear out faster due to my inefficient movements, as well as the fact I was generally run down due to my continued heavy use of alcohol.

But towards the end of 2008 and the start of January 2009, my feet began to feel always ice cold, as well as having severe bouts of pins and needles. I realised something was very wrong when one Saturday evening in mid-January I went to stand up from my office chair and simply collapsed physically unable to get up, requiring assistance of paramedics to get back onto my chair.

Even as my mobility radically deteriorated over the next few days, I had no idea what was going on and my current GP was no help at all. I managed from the local council to get a hoist installed so I could get in and out of bed and what was happening was certainly not getting any better. Then one Saturday at the end of January I was sitting at my computer as I could feel a sense of numbness rising up my body to just above a navel area, and this is when I called an ambulance and got myself to hospital.

It was fortunate that I had gone to the hospital when I did has it turned out that I had an acute nerve virus that mirrored the symptoms of Gullian-Barre Syndrome and if I had waited any longer to get to hospital, I could had required incubation to assist with my breathing, which would have potentially caused further serious complications. As soon as I got to hospital and I had the initial tests, I was quickly put on a strong dose of antibiotics taken intravenously for about a week.

I remained in hospital for about ten days and I had assumed from what the doctors had been saying that once I had finished the antibiotics, the worse would be over. I knew I would not be fighting fit as soon as I was discharged from hospital but I had assumed it would be simply a few days of rest and lots of TLC before I would be back to normal. The reality was however very different as I realised that I was not at the end of my recovery but actually at the start of a lengthy process to literally get myself back on my feet.

Because I was eager to get out of hospital and the hospital had assumed I was already set up for a level of need that was not the case, I was provided with very little information and simply told that a physiotherapist from Neuro-Rehab team would contact me in due course, which I had assumed would be simply a matter of days. The reality was I actually needed a lot more support after I had been discharged and none of this had been put in place.

The fundamental issue was that I needed support overnight since I was now completely immobile and experiencing a lot of incontinence and other issues. While Stefan, who was my volunteer at the time, was happy to assist me in the short term, it is not something he could do in the long-term as something had to be done. Stefan, Flora and myself seemed to begin to act as a family unit as I was locked out of the system that was supposed to be supporting me with my recovery, trying desperately to break back in, and in the end, succeeding.

This is the start of the most craziest period of my life due to the immense stress of being bombarded with an endless stream of health professionals now interfering with my life whether I liked it or not. Despite being extremely unwell to the point I was almost catatonic most of the day, I had to remain alert of the complex politics being paid around me with people trying to make decisions about my life, sometimes against my will.

Despite talk of temporary putting me in a care home, I summoned up the determination and political will power to get what I needed. I managed to secure the overnight support I needed for as long as I needed it but it was not without its fair share of problems and hassle. During the few months I had overnight support, I managed to go through three different care agencies. Each agency presented their own set of problems and because my long experience of having social care, I was able to easily see the mistakes they were making and inform them of them in a manner many other users would not be able to do.

After some battles with council and health services, I had a few weeks support from an intermediate care physiotherapist before being referred to the Community Neurorehab team who supported me for the rest of my recovery. This was a great team led in my case by a fantastic physiotherapist, Claire, who basically helped me to learn to walk again understanding I needed to keep the gait I was used to a someone with cerebral palsy.

I really liked the team and I found it to be a very positive experience because they were very outcome focused and they allowed me to set my own goals and outcomes. They were prepared to support me for as long as I felt I needed and that enabled many issues around my cerebral palsy that had never been dealt with before, as well as the nerve virus and my general health, to be sorted. This was the retuning of a lifestyle.

A long time effect from the nerve virus was that I now had long term chronic pain issues. This required me to take three types of painkillers on an ongoing basis; gabipentin, ibuprofen and dihydrocodine. While my ability to manage my pain has improved slowly over the years since I had the nerve virus. Because I am unable to swallow tablets, I have them crushed up and put in soda, which has now become an every day part of my routine.

The nerve virus, as well as stopping my use of alcohol, with the assistance of my gp and the neurorehab team, meant this was a good time to explore other medication that could improve my general quality of life. This included using a low dosage of Bacoflen, which is a muscle relaxant that is commonly used by people with cerebral palsy. I also started medication that improved my sleeping and my mental health.

As a part of this general review of my whole health situation was a proper chance to explore my mental health issues, which as I have mentioned before I probably had throughout my life. This was when I was properly diagnosed with cyclothymia, a form of mild bipolar that meant I experienced rapid periods of mania and depression, where I could feel that I was experiencing both extremes at the same time. Now I could understand my condition I could manage it better. Having a label and an explanation enabled me to track my mood better and understand why I may be feeling a specific way at a specific time, enabling me to better manage my stress and mental wellbeing in general.

The whole episode of my nerve virus may have appeared to be a major tragedy in my life, but it was actually a major step forward for me in rebuilding my life after the years of misery from the initial actions of Helen Tyers. Importantly, it saw me cease from using alcohol for the time being and therefore I recovered my sleeping pattern as well as my health in general. It would not be the end of my health issues but it certainly went a long way to improving them. While I was able to walk again at home, my outdoor mobility had deteriorated from the nerve virus and so I was now using an electric wheelchair when I went out.

The six month of absolute chaos that I experienced took me to a new level of uncertainty that resulting in myself becoming stronger as a person. By a willingness to work hard and make the most of the recovery process, I gained a new level of stability in all aspects of my life as I had the opportunity to be truly happy with myself and where I was going. I was now reaching the end of a journey that had started with Helen Tyers and I was now going to a more positive place.

29 Balsy with cerebral palsy

I always wanted to be on television and over the years I have managed to well and truly achieve this goal. In 1995, I appeared briefly in a BBC1 documentary on disability discrimination called 'Invisible Walls'. Then in the same year I appeared on ITV's News at Ten about a court case in the UK relating to the euthanasia of a boy with cerebral palsy. During that day, I had been frustrated at the news in the daytime and there was no opinion from someone with a impairment so I rang ITN and said "Why don't you interview me", and they did!

My greatest exploration into the world of television has got to be my regular appearance as a star of Channel 4's disability themed prank show called I'm Spazticus. This is about disabled actors, including myself, playing pranks on an unsuspecting general public. I feel privileged to have been involved in the show from the beginning in terms of being an actor, staring in the pilot as well as both series.

I becoma involved with the show because I was on the books of a disabled modelling agency. In 1999, from the email that came via Scope I found myself going to a castings to model for a newspaper advert for a government campaign about the Disability Discrimination Act called 'See the Person'. I was successful in getting the role and I appeared in a number of national newspapers in October 1999.

As a part of doing this piece of work, I joined the modelling agency. I however did not receive any work from the agency until December 2004, when I was sent to the auditions for the I'm Spazticus pilot, which was called Dystopia at this time. I knew that the audition was at Channel Four in London, and so I assumed it was at the main building but it was actually at another building, which made me late for my audition.

This did not seem to matter because as soon as the director, Jamie O'Leary, met me we immediately got on and he quickly saw that I had a good sense of humour and I was comfortable with the camera that fitting well into what work he was looking for. So while my audition was short, it was also successful as I was offered a part in the pilot. I was also personally pleased because at the auditions there was another more established comedian with cerebral palsy, Laurence Clarke, waiting and we were probably going for the same part, which I ended up getting.

The I'm Spazticus pilot was a part of then annual series of comedy pilots under the banner 'Comedy Lab', which has over the years produced a number of successful comedies that went on to one or more series. This meant the budgets were low and the material possible was edgy as this was late night television. Jamie had recruited a number of different actors representing different impairment groups.

My part of the pilot was filmed in freezing February 2005, and consisted of three parts where only one part made it to the final cut. The first part of the filming with interviewing people on the Red Carpet, asking then strange questions to see if they would simply answer them due to my speech impairments. That was certainly a cold evening standing outside but I got to see a lot of celebrities including Kylie Minogue.

The next day in the morning I was filming at London Fashion Week and this is the piece you can see in the finished pilot. Then we did some filming production offices which again never went anywhere. I will still walking at the time and we were travelling all together in a car from location to location since it was a small crew. There was a real camaraderie which I really enjoyed.

The pilot was first broadcast in May 2005 with mixed reviews. This was indeed a divisive show with the title of the show causing controversy before people even began watching the show. I however loved the title because it matched the sense of humour the show was trying to portray. People also complained that the show was mocking people with impairments but it was instead mocking people without impairments!

The show did not make it to series at that time for various reasons and so as a late night show few people watched because it was before the era of on demand, the show slowly faded into the mists of time. As a forgotten show, I decided a few years later, as no one was interested in its copyright, I would put the pilot on youtube myself so it could have a new international audience. And for now, the story of I'm Spazticus had ended.

In 2006, Jamie asked me to be involved with a new show he was working on called Taboogie for E4, reviving my role from I'm Spazticus. The show was a multiple minority group prank show dealing with gender, race, sexuality and of course disability, which is where I came in. As a part of the show, I interviewed the famous gay rights activist, Peter Tatchell, in a manner similar to Ali G, asking questions like 'if there are gay rights, are there gay wrongs?'. Like I'm Spasticus, Taboogie was a one off show that did not go anywhere.

And that is it, I'm Spazticus was a part of television history and something that sadly never went to series. Then in 2012, 7 years after the pilot had been broadcasted, everything changed. Channel 4 was now the Paralympic broadcaster for the London games, and it had a healthy budget for a range of disability themed programmes including a comedy. This meant that finally I'm Spazticus had been commissioned into a series of 4x30mins shows as well as a 5th Best bits show. This was fantastic news.

Jamie asked a lot of the cast from the pilot to return, including myself, and we embarked on a new chapter and something many of us did not believe would happen. I was now an electric wheelchair user, as well as using a communication aid to compliment my speech. I had a wide range of roles in the show which included being a living silver statue, a pearly king and a breakdancer. There was more filming for myself and so more pay! It was very hard work but very rewarding and a lot of fun to do.

My favourite scene of the series was the police line up of 3 people who had real cp, including myself, and one unsuspecting member of the public each time who had been asked to act like he had cerebral palsy to fill the line up. This bizarre situation was so funny to film as well as to watch, and it was what the show was all about, pushing the boundaries.

The first series was broadcasted over 4 consecutive nights in August 2012, and like the pilot it had mixed reviews from the traditional media and social media. It remained a very divisive show which people with or without impairments either liked or hated. Despite this, it did not stop the show being commissioned again for a second series.

With a bigger budget, cast and crew, I was once against proud to be a part of this phoneme. The new director of the show, as Jamie as taken a backseat, had recognised the variety of my acting talent and I appeared to have a greater role in the show with bigger pranks as one of the main cast members. There were 2 specific pranks that stood out for me.

The first was called 'money for a disabled person' which was a very simple. One disabled actor would pretend to have a stand raising money for a disabled person. As soon as anyone gave them any money, I would rush onto the scene pretending they had just brought me as 'a disabled person' as I would ask them about where do we live and what are we having for tea, following them off camera until a member of the crew caught up with them and signed them off as okay for broadcast.

The second prank of the rap video that included the lyrics; 'I'm Big, I'm Balsy, I am the rebel with cerebral palsy', which has become a catchphrase for myself. This was great fun to film and as you will see in the episode I love the reaction of the music critics being asked for their opinion. I have never seen anyone's eyes pop out as much as when they see my rap video, I think it is one of the best highlights of the series.

I was always proud to be a part of what still remains a revolutionary and divisive show, that fitted in well to my own story and the way I saw the world. It also showed that I was able to put my mind to anything and I feel honoured to have been able to have such a diverse range of experiences in my life.

30 A tweetful experience

As we entered the 2010s, social media was playing a bigger part in my life and especially Twitter. It had taken me a long time to get the hang of Twitter but I found it was a good way to get my viewpoint across to a wider audience. As the years went by, Twitter would play an increasingly greater role in my whole marketing strategy for myself and my work. It was an immense tool which would really assist me, but as I would find out, it also had its problems including a darker side.

The 2010s, and in particularly the election of the coalition government in May 2010, saw a major shift in the make up, demands and attitudes of the vocal disability movement, and I would find myself increasingly having a different opinion to other disabled activists. For me, the whole focus of the disability movement, if there was such a thing, had moved from a broad wide of issues about social issues to simply be focused around welfare issues in a very negative way. I also felt the voice of disabled people had been hijacked by the anti-cuts and therefore anti-Tory left wing movement.

I fundamentally believed in unconditional self-worth where everyone without exception has human potential and the ability to work, and the ability to make some kind of meaningful contribution to society, accepting that this did not always equate to being able to earn enough to live on without financial assistance from the state. For myself, it was a very simple and uncontroversial statement. I slowly understood from my dialogues with other activists on twitter that few of them actually properly agreed with me.

My many dialogues with activists on the subjects related to human potential and how framing disabled people as simply a welfare issues quickly turned to arguments and then personal attacks on myself which my general nature would not allow myself to simply walk away from. I too often ended up in fits of rage in the comfort of my own home as I became frustrated at not being able to express myself quick enough and fully enough within the restrictions of twitter.

I was always a straight talker and I never minded someone disagreeing with me if they had a valid point to make but because people were too often unable to constructively disagree with what I was saying, I was too often simply insulted and I was often foolish enough to fight back ending up with me simply being blocked as a hollow victory for them. It was always often assumed that because I appeared to disagree with their left wing viewpoint on issues that I must simply be a Tory, which was not the case. These mindless activists wrapped up in post-truth headlines could not understand I was developing a deep analytical overview of the issues involved far removed from party politics.

The major area of concern many other activists had expressed related to the new way various disability benefits were being assessed by private contractors, particularly in terms of ATOS, which has received a lot of criticism. One of the concerns raised was the level of fear and stress the assessment process which I felt may relate to poor communication in terms of how can letters and other documents were written. I had always been someone that if I saw a problem I would try to fix it, and in that context, I contacted ATOS to see if I could help. I had one unpaid meeting with them to discuss the issues which did not go anywhere.

A couple of things happened together around August 2013 which resulted in an explosive mixture. Firstly, I had a love/hate relationship with a disability journalist called John Pring who provided a voice for many of the activists I was now endlessly disagreeing with, including himself, on his website called Disability News Service. After a brief discussion with him, I agreed to write a blog for his site to why I wanted to worked for ATOS on a foolish assumption that people would understand my position.

The second thing was that because of a vague remark someone had made about myself in an article they had written in the Huffington Post, I had successfully won the opportunity to write a response article that gave me the further opportunity to write for the Huffington Post on a mostly weekly basis as I still do. I had been previously frustrated that other activists were giving the opportunity to write in National newspapers, mainly the Guardian, and that I did not have the opportunity to put my differing views across. My first article was what I saw at the key urban myths had been created about ATOS and the assessment process which did not ring true logically, which really did not go down very well with almost 100 comments.

The final thing was earlier in the year I had applied and was successful in receiving financial assistance from a charity, Leonard Cheshire Disability, to attend the Labour Party conference to assist my campaigning on various disability rated issues. I saw this as a private thing that was not that particularly special as I was not representing anyone but myself. However, when it became public knowledge it caused somewhat of a stir amongst other activists and there were a number of complaints made as I refused to agree with them as well as fought back, which appeared to be spearheaded by John Pring. Without allowing me to put my side of the story across the charity cancelled their assistance, which meant I could not attend. I however went to the conference the following year using my own finances.

These 3 events combined to cause what could only be describe as an explosion of abuse towards me on social media. There were also an endless supply of blog written about myself full of insults and misinformation. If you were to believe everything that was being said about me at that time you would believe I was a Tory Boy who was being paid a large amount of money (I wish) by the Conservative Party to upset and annoy other activists. I worked for ATOS with a well paid job (again I wish) to assist them in killing other people with impairments. I was a traitor to disabled people who tried to misrepresent everyone. And the best one of all was I was the love child of Iain Duncan Smith! Much of the abuse bordered onto harassment and if I fought back, which was my nature to do, I was attacked further as I could do nothing right in their paranoid eyes. I was also disheartened as a lot of the insults I received were mental health related, saying I was irrational and crazy, etc. Whether or not they knew about my mental health issues, I still found their comments slightly hurtful.

It was clearly a very difficult time for me emotionally as I remained deeply frustrated and angry with the situation. I was witnessing real post-truth myths being created right in front of my eyes and it was about myself as I saw this cruel game of Chinese whispers being played through social media. Most of the people who were attacking me had never met me and certainly had no clue or no interesting about who I really was, they were simply a part of the pack of hounds out for blood, targeting anyone disagreeing with their viewpoint.

People like John Pring and other activists who knew me were better than their followers but they allowed the mindless sheep looking for someone to blame for everything wrong to their lives to carry on with their campaign of hatred, with the activists pretending to have the morale high ground as they endlessly fuelled the flames. I think many of the activists who did know me and understanding some of what I was saying where actually fearful of me as they know I was making sense with my differing views. I also believe many of them were jealous about the fact I was confident to have my own opinion. This meant it was in the best interest of the disability movement, who I believe were actually dependent on keeping people with impairments dependent and disempowered, to endlessly try to discredit my viewpoint.

The division between myself and other activists has remained to this point and has probably become stronger. If people understand my views properly then I would understand that I am not really that interested in party politics but rather the details of specific and complex issues, solving real issues for real people. If something did not make sense because half the picture was missing then I wanted to know the whole picture so I could make sense of it.

I did not mind being regarded as an outcast to other activists as I was developing my own complex understanding of the world, carving out my own story, and better understanding what the difference I could make to the world. The abuse I received in 2013 simply made me stronger and more able to defend myself from unfounded attacks. It also made be more committed to my vision of the world and my desire to assist other people with impairments to be enabled and empowered to make a meaningful contribution to society in a manner that fitted into their own unique wonderful stories. I was becoming as strong as I have ever been because of what I had experienced.

31 Finding the real me

By the end of 2013 and the start of 2014 I was starting to feel very good about myself and where I was going. The problems which had been started by Helen Tyers was now ten years ago and it was completely over and I felt that for the most part I had everything I had before, and plenty more. My home suited my needs at that specific time, my personal support was working well with Flora and my current volunteer Matt, I had a good relationship with Patrick, my financial situation was reasonably okay and I had various pieces of work.

One of my main focuses at the time was to increase my reputation and influence by firstly increasing the number of twitter followers I had, and secondly I would ensure I wrote a typical disability-themed weekly blog in the Huffington Post whenever I could. In terms of increasing my twitter followers, after trying some advertising, I hit upon the simply ide` of following as many people and organisations related to disability and other issues as I could and then asking those who have not already followed me back to follow me back with a message saying "I would be extremely honoured if you would follow me back". While a few people have found this annoying, it has overall worked extremely as I have currently reached 20000 followers, which is a mighty good achievement. I am also pleased because it is far more than most of the activists who try to discredit me, including John Pring.

Ås I have said previously, while I have managed to acquire a lot of work over the years, working with almost 200 organisations in one way or another, I had always found it difficult to maintain long term financial stability which I am still looking for as I write this story. I have believed for a long time and still believe that I am going to achieve that goal at some point, and that I am going to find what I refer to currently as my golden egg, that project, service or working relationship which will make me financial stable and comfortable in the way I wish for the rest of my life.

I have learnt what I call my products and services are simply indications of what I can achieve for any potential customer, and that my one and only real product I have always been selling is myself. I am providing customers with my experiences, my expertise and most importantly my unique perspective of a whole range of issues. I think this is regardless of how big or small my customer is, whether it be a small start up or the BBC, the details of the work I have provided have been born out of negotiations as opposed to any form of tendering process. I have tried to apply for work that has been tendered out and it has rarely been successful because people either wish me to work for them or they don't, it has been that simple.

SInce I am the product, it means that in order to find the golden egg with my name on I am now so desperate to find, I need to be able to attract myself to whoever has that egg. This is difficult as because of the variety of my work and the wide range of skills I have, the egg could come in any shape in the way all my work has been, so the owner of them will need to know the as much as possible about what I am able to do as possible to catch their attention as a potential supplier. This all means I need to be very good at marketing myself.

My marketing and promotion strategy has been something less formal and ad-hoc including my use of social media, my blogs, my Wikipedia page and my website. My website is the most important element as since this is my formal shop window to the world, my best opportunity to sell myself to anyone who wanted to know about myself, my skills, my achievements and my views

I have had a website for many years and I have always refreshed my site completely every few years, especially when I have changed the software I was using to design the website. I have also always designed the website myself because I wished to remain in control of the site as much as possible and be able to change it and add bits when I wanted to with immediate affect without having to be dependent on a designer,

In learning to design my own website, I have needed to understand what content I have needed to put on the website to sell myself. This has meant over the years I have slowly learn more about myself and how to present that to the outside world. While that may sound easy, when you lead a busy and hectic life, it can be hard to pause for a moment and actually take some time to understand who you really are. Writing this story has been another of moment to peace and have a real think about my life, putting many of my experiences on paper, which has been an exhausting exercise.

I am amazed sometimes how easily I have forgotten parts of my life including some of the organisations I have worked with, which can be very frustrating when you normally have a very good short term and long term memory. Now whenever I remember something like an organisation I have worked with, or an idea for a new product or lead, I write it down on my computer as soon as I can. I have learnt to become very organised in this way and I think this is because working for myself for so long I had to become strict with myself as someone always managing my own time.

Despite what some people now think about me, I have always been open and honest about myself as well as always happy to answer any questions people may have about myself truthfully, even personal ones, as I do not see any reason to do anything different. If you ask my opinion on a specific issue then I will give a straight answer even if that is not what you wish to hear.

I also felt had someone already damaged by the pressures of including myself in society, often when I was not wanted, I found that I could do my bit for other people with impairments by being the 'show house' for our issues and feelings so other people with impairments, especially younger people, could enjoy more privacy in that context than I have ever experienced. Real privacy is something I have never had so I am not even sure I know what it is.

And I believe this desire to be a permanent educational case study is why I have evolved my website into an ever growing open house of who I am as someone with significant impairments who wishes to make a substantial meaningful contribution to society. I have often been accused of being egotistical because of my website and other self-promotional activities but this is how I gain customers to make a living.

I do believe that I have built up a vast amount of power and influence over the years in my fields of work but as I said at the beginning of the story, I do not believe I am no more or less important than anyone else. If I disagree with anyone, whether they are my personal assistant, a neighbour, the Queen, the Pope or even god himself, I will tell them straight, as well as if I actually did agree with them. As I have said before, I do not see any reason to be anything different. I believe this is why some people are frightened by me, because I am so honest as well as the fact I know what I am talking about. If I do not know something, I will say and then look on Google to find out more about whatever it is.

I believe this shows a level of confidence in myself and my belief system few people truly have. I believe I know myself, I am happy with myself, I like myself and most importantly, I love myself and everything that comes with that. I have no regrets, there is nothing about my current situation I would change that is not already on my evolving journey towards an ever improving life. I am able to always see the positive and I have always found it strange when I have been criticised for this, often by people who have sadly not found happiness within themselves.

But maintaining happiness and striving for something better is always a constant battle and one where I can not afford to become lax or complacent about because while there may be rewards on the way, true happiness is about constantly working towards the next goal.

32 The final move

By 2015, I was well and truly settled at Everdon Road, or so I believed. I was starting to have a few niggles that were growing. The stairs up to my flat were not a major problem but for the long term, it was not something that was ideal. Having the stairs also meant that Patrick and other friends or colleagues with mobility problems could not visit me if they wanted to, which was okay but it was still a niggle.

The main concern related to my electric chair which I was now using most of the time when I went out. After a lot of negotiation with Access to Work, I got my first electric wheelchair in August 2011. Because of the stairs to my flat, I could not bring my wheelchair into my flat, and so as a part of the package from Access to Work, I had a cupboard built in the communal area downstairs to store the cupboard.

This was working great until 2014, when Whitefrairs, my social housing landlord, had to upgrade the fire regulations in the block's communal area, that included a non-smoking ban, and the removal of any fire hazards, which included the cupboard for my wheelchair! Whitefrairs were very good about this, and at their own expense, they provided me with another storage cupboard out in the communal backyard, including the power supply needed to charge the chair.

This was all great but the solution was specifically designed for mobility scooters, not electric wheelchairs, and I am sure that the fact my wheelchair was now spending most of its time outside, especially during the winter months, was not doing it any good as the power of the battery was now reducing. I was also starting to become unhappy at how long it was taking to get the wheelchair ready which was making it difficult when I was ordering a taxi, when to make the call etc. I also did not like having to get in the wheelchair and having my belts fastened outside in the winter months. I knew this was not an ideal situation in the long term and that eventually, something had to be done.

By the spring and summer of 2015, my wheelchair was metaphorically on its last legs and it was time to look at getting a new chair. Access to Work had been through a lot of changes and it was going to be more difficult to obtain a new chair from them, and I was unhappy that they did not pay for repairs. The idea solution was to try to obtain an electric wheelchair was my local NHS wheelchair service, which I had tried previously and was unsuccessful with.

So, I had a meeting in May or June of that year with the NHS wheelchair service, The fundamental problem was that in order to be eligible for an electric wheelchair, I had to be able to use it indoors as well as outside, and I had to be able to bring the chair inside my own property, which I clearly could not do at this time. During our conversation one of the assessors gently asked if I had considered moving to a more accessible flat in a way where they appeared to be expecting me to hit the roof. I thought for a moment before saying 'well yes, I think I will move'.

While I had not consciously thought about moving up to this point, it all suddenly made perfect sense. Getting a new electric wheelchair was critical to my long term mobility, and this was the only way I was going to get one. It also gave me a once in a decade or so opportunities to resolve a few other issues. This included the opportunity to downgrade from three bedrooms to two, and so avoid the bedroom tax, especially since I was not really using my lounge at all compared to many years ago. I would simply merge my lounge and office into a single room.

So, I started social housing hunting and filled out all the relevant forms, including the form for specially adapted housing. I had assumed at this point that I would have to choose between having a good central location in the city or having a fully accessible place. I knew that having an accessible place was the 'right' thing to do in the long term but I was not keen on the idea of living isolated on the outskirts of the city. This is why I was really pleased and surprised when I received a phone call from Orbit Housing offering a place that was fully accessible and in the centre of the city.

21 Stoney Stanton Road, where I am now currently now and on the same road I was living on some 20 years ago, is a spacious two bedroom fully accessible ground floor flat that is just opposite Coventry's main NHS walk-in centre, that houses a range of health services, and next to the wonderful and beautiful Swanswell Park. This place had everything I needed for my immediate future as well as my long-term needs including if my needs once again suddenly increased like with the nerve virus.

The place did however have a few downsides. The first was I could not leave any of my windows open for any length of time because I was living on the ground floor in what was a very public place. However, connected to my back door, I had a covered caged area with a locked gate, making it completely safe to leave my back door wide open in the summer. The back door also gave access to the car park which was great for deliveries and when we had workman doing stuff.

Another problem with the flat was that it had storage heaters instead of central heating, which was something I simply had to get used to. I quickly discovered that it has very difficult to manage and so within a couple of months I had purchased new heaters for my bedroom and office, which were expensive but they did enable me to properly control my heating so that I did not get too warm or too cold, which was very important.

A final problem with the flat that was not something I discovered until the winter was a lot of homeless people, who were mostly drug addicts, choose to use my communal hallway as a shelter most nights to sleep as well as their 'activities'. During 2016, the problem has persisted with the housing association, Orbit Housing, trying a number of things to sort the problem like a more secure front door, with slow progress.

The move into the flat was as stressful as any move can be with its fair share of minor complications but overall, it went extremely well with no major problems. Over the last 18 months, I settled in nicely into the flat, which with a good combination of existing and new furniture, can meet any possible need I may have now or in the future. I feel that I am now extremely settled in my home life to a level I have not been before.

I love so much about the flat in terms of its size and accessibility, especially as I certainly did not miss the third bedroom from Everdon Road. I love where the flat so near to the city centre and in easy walking to the train station, theatre, cinema, many restaurants and so much more. I love the fact I live opposite the main health centre where the walk in centre, my GP, my dentist and many other services are based. I love that outside my office window is a view of the park with its trees and lake, with changing scenery according to the seasons. I love having to walk through the park to get to and from the city centre, and being able to chase the swans, geese, ducks, pigeons and other birds so domesticated that they simply waddle out my way unfazed.

Despite it not being the mansion I once dreamed of having, it is the place I feel I deserve as someone with a significant impairments and live-in volunteers who was in their early forties. It was a decent and respectful place that had everything I could possibly need and it would be something I would have purchased if I had that kind of money and was not eligible for social housing, this was not some kind of compromise to what I really wanted. Also, there were no obvious niggles that there was with any previous property, I can truly see myself living here for the rest of my life regardless of how my situation my change, this was a home, my home, that is I believe future-proof for whatever life has in store me next and in the future.

33 Reaching the top

The story has now reached 2016 and it is time to reflect on what achieved and what I had become as someone aged 42, a leading disability consultant with a range of impairments including cerebral palsy. Had I become the person I wanted to become? And was I happy with how that person was? These were questions it was now time to answer.

I believe that I have benefited immensely from the development and growth of technology, the internet and most recently, social media. These have been phenomenon of my lifetime, changing society and the way people interact in a manner we would think unthinkable in the 1970s. I had made the most of technology, riding the edge of innovation as a key factor in my liberation from the physical and other impairment related barriers that existed in the past.

Social media especially had not only providing me with a voice but also a sense of authority as my twitter followers have risen to over 20000 as I write this, which is impressive for someone who would not be considered a celebrity. In April 2016, the Birmingham Post newspaper named me as a part of their Power 250 for being one of ten most influential people in social media within the West Midlands. This was a mainstream Power list, not just about people with impairments, and I believe the specific category was based on statistical analysis as opposed to just judgment.

If examining this achievement with where I have come from, it is pretty amazing. I believe platforms like Twitter has fundamentally changed social order, redefining culture and status for the 21st century. People are now less interested in what car you drive and more interested in how many twitter followers you have. I am under no illusion that the number of twitter followers or facebook friends I have been in any way related to serious and meaningful friendships, not all of them at least. They are a power base to assist my influence as a dysability consultant and entrepreneur to grow in a way that would previously have been impossible.

It is very clear to me that I have become very well-know within my fields of work and activism, primarily disability and social care, even if I am not well liked. I believe most of the key players know or have heard of me, and I know or have heard of them. It has taken myself a long time and a lot of networking over many years to reach this point. I also have many less known contacts in many organisations, and I know how to find out the people I need to know in specific organisations as well as how to communicate with them in an effective manner.

I feel like someone who metaphorically has a lot of different weapons at my disposal. I feel that I am able to do anything that I truly put my mind into achieving as I am always willing and able with confidence to find out whatever I need to know to overcome any barriers that are in the way of achieving my end goal. If I need to make a complaint about something to put it right, I am able to do this with confidence in a manner that is professional and effective.

I am very aware that the extent of my influence is not always obvious, concrete or tangible and therefore not often recognised within a public arena. Adding to the fact that many of my views have been less than mainstream in recent years, I can understand when I am deliberately overlooked for things like the Power 100 of the top 100 most influential disabled people in the UK. But does it matter as I know I am and the influence I have? And how it assists many people in many ways, and often in ways even I can not realise or understand. I am the turtle that won the race of my bigger picture by being slow and steady.

I believe I am an agent of change and live up to the real meaning of being an activist. I see many people who call themselves activists simply spending most of their day posting mostly anti-government rhetoric masked as concerns for issues, and then attacking anyone who disagrees with them as they feel a part of a collective view where everyone who is morally right agrees with, and those who disagree are morally wrong. Within this era of urban myths and post truths plaguing modern politics and modern activism, there is little room for real debate. As I have said previously, whenever I have tried to debate issues with many activists on Twitter they have simply tried to drag it back to simplified party politics.

For myself, activism is helping real people on the ground. It is firstly about listening to individuals not just in terms of what they say but also digging deeper to establish what they actually mean, which they may need help expressing. It is then about enabling them to understand all the options they have available and finally to facilitate them to action their choices without judgment. Activism is also able putting things right by communicating effectively with the relevant organisations effectively because it needs to be done without worrying if anyone else has done the same, as oppose to getting people to sign petitions and make long whingeing blogs.

I met him in April 2014 when he had just started in his post. It was quite amusing when I arrived to the meeting and the receptionist called up and said He also does not yet have his own Twitter account, so I beat him on that score.

While I have done really well to achieve this high in my fields of work, I still have further to go because I am not finished or feel completely satisfied. It is not only about having financial stability but also validation and recognition for the major contributions I have done. I am aware that to achieve this in a manner that does not conform to how others wish me to behave, I will need to go that extra mile and really make myself impossible to ignore in a good way. While I do feel it is important to provoke people to think outside their comfort zones, I do not intend to harm people.

I want to show people the right way of being things by practising what I am preaching, something I always try to do. It does not mean I believe I am perfect, that I have the moral high ground, or that I can't enjoy life, but I am exactly what you see. I can lie or falsely smile out of respect for others, but I do not believe I am ever two faced, I have always felt that was a waste of the often limited energy I had. I have always found the truth to often be my greatest weapon, and it often the thing that other people feared the most despite the fact I was never frightened.

Throughout my adult life, I had steadily and slowly grown my power and influence to the point I have at currently, and I will slowly and steadily grow it further until a point where I am satisfied that I have made the difference to the world that my life has been about, even if I do not precisely know what that is at this point in time. I can only ever do my best and so long as I keep doing my best than I am doing well. Life is for living and I believed I lived my life well and I hope to continue that.

After many difficult years, I feel strong and confident about where I am and where I am going. I have achieved so much already in my lifetime, far more than most people, but that there is still a lot more for me to achieve personally and professionally to improve my own life experiences and opportunities, as well as those of others.

34 Heading towards peace

I found 2016 to be a hard year for a number of reasons that related to stress, alcohol and my health. However, towards the end of the year everything had settled down to provide me with time to write this story, and to prepare for what currently appears to be a positive future ahead.

The stress I experienced started very early on in the year and related to my regular review of Access to Work. I had a short break in January with a close friend in Budapest which was supposed to relax me but I received an email from Access to Work on my way to Heathrow Airport as I was staying overnight in London demanding I contact them asap or I risked using my funding, which was 30 hours of my support each week!

The problem turned out to be they have changed the rules without informing anyone, and now if you were self employed, you had to be earning a minimum level of turnover to receive support from them. This was frustrating for myself because while I had power and influence in my fields of work, this did not easily equate to paid work. Everyone is happy for me to work with them, as I have a lot of skills to offer, but not many people actually want to pay for them.

After a few worrying and stressful weeks, the matter was resolved by sheer luck as opposed to anything else, but it came at a price in terms of my physical and emotional health. I had not had a proper holiday since I had been on wonderful Caribbean cruse with Patrick in January 2015, primarily because my resources had with absorbed with the costs of moving, which was also a stressful and exhausting venture. This had already left me by physically and emotionally weaker. The result of all this was that I once again hit the bottle in a big way.

I had starting drinking socially for a year or so, and it appeared to be manageable but the stress of Access to Work and the absolute fear of potentially losing Flora as my personal assistant had pushed me into a temporarily period of weakness and vulnerability that saw my use of alcohol spiral out of control. Once the emotional need for alcohol ended, it simply became a chemical addiction that I was unable to stop.

This time I knew that I needed help and I managed to secure assistance from a local alcohol support service who provided home visits on a weekly to fortnightly basis. Due to my chemical dependency and my fear of the withdrawal symptoms in an uncontrolled environment, I was finding it difficult to reduce my level of alcohol usage. It was therefore agreed that I should embark on a residential detox programme and so it was a matter of waiting, and staying safe, while this could be arranged. Fate would however choose a different course of action for myself.

In June my left foot started to swell to an uncomfortable size which was now affecting my indoor mobility. There was initial concern that it may be a Deep Vein Trombonist but that was ruled out as the foot continued to swell. In the end, I went to A&E at the local hospital and I was admitted for a significant foot infection. I knew that being in hospital meant that I would not be able or allowed to continue to consume alcohol and so I was very upfront about my situation and I would need help with detoxing.

It transpired that I would be in hospital for 3 weeks and that my foot infection has been a result of my alcohol usage and while my liver was not so far damaged, it was seriously ill. This firstly meant no more alcohol ever again which was something I was 100% committed to, as it had never been put in those terms previously. With a lot of tests, a lot of blood taking and a lot of medications, my liver showed signs of recovery and by my outpatients appointment in October, my liver had fully recovered and I had been discharged. This was a final last chance to get things right in terms of my health.

As always, it was not quite that simple because exactly a week after I was discharged from hospital in July, I was admitted again onto the same ward with an unrelated case of e.coli, which is a very bad blood infection requiring another week in hospital. Clearly after almost the whole of the summer in hospital, it took myself another month or so to fully recover and get used to my new lifestyle completely free of alcohol.

While 2016 was a hard year in terms of my health, it was also a productive year in terms of sorting out my back office and my marketing strategies. While this year and the previous year had been quiet work wise for myself because of moving and my health issues, I was also using the time to prepare for a major 'comeback' in 2017. As well as writing this story, as a piece of therapy as well as an opportunity to show the world by inner workings, using new software, WIX, I had provided my website a brand new look with more information about myself. I had now built the website in a manner where it could be quickly amended and expanded. During early 2017, I also plan a gradual and carefully craft a new image for myself exploring properly all the features of my graphics software.

I have recently looked in detail at how to describe myself and how I see the complex psychological and sociological images that exist in discussing people with impairments. In trying to show that I have a new way of thinking about issues, I decided to adopt the term Dysability. Where disability means a lack of ability, dysability means a difficulty in ability, that can be overcome with appropriate changes, assistance and support. This is more in line with an advanced understanding of the social model and represents a new era of understanding. It is a term that I am still developing and currently I am not entirely confident in using the term of every occasion but that I now have the breathing space and influence to carve a unique profile for myself. I also for selfish reasons decided to start using the term so The last few years have been about the last few pieces of my jigsaw puzzle together in terms of my personal life, my home life and my health so that I have more time and a better opportunity to focus on the one thing I have yet to fully achieve, which is financial stability and long term satisfying paid and meaningful work, that golden egg that I have previously talked about. I always say next year is going to be the year as that is something I have to believe and I need to believe. Without hope and positivity, what else do I have?

Going forward, I do feel that I am finally heading towards peace with myself by becoming the person I always wanted to be and maybe I was always destined to be. I had overcome so many barriers to reach this point in my life and I fully understand that I am going to have to overcome a whole new set of often unexpected challenges in order to reach my final goal at some point in the future.

I am not sure even now I know or understand what that final goal is or whether it something tangible or something vague. It could be a combination of a number of things like being happy with myself and at peace with how I have become. The point is I am committed to keep focused on reaching that final goal in the everything I do. The golden egg will simply be a faster means of transport to that goal as opposed to the goal itself, and I may need a number of golden eggs at different points in my future to be able to achieve everything I would like.

This commitment shows that while I may be at peace with my current place on my personal journey, and my current place in society, I still have great determination and real fire in my belly to move forward, going in any direction I need to take, understanding there is no detailed map to my final goal. But as I understand how a series of seemingly random events have assisted me to reach this in time, I am very aware that another series of seemingly random events is waiting to challenge me and assist me in something that is part fate and part self-determination, where I never likely to know or understand which is which, but is this not what makes life exciting and worth living?

35 What is my future?

As we have finally reached the end of my story in terms of the past and the present, it is now time to have a brief exploration into my potential future and how things may develop as I go from here into my fifties, sixties and beyond in relations to a range of issues based on my current understanding and knowledge.

In terms of housing, I am extremely settled at 21 Stoney Stanton Road and I can not see myself ever wanted to move to this place, or indeed every needing to move from here unless it was somehow forcibly taken away from me like an eviction or devastating fire. I would need an incredibly amazing job offer with a stupidly large salary, like in 7 digit figures, for me to consider moving, and certainly consider from Coventry. With the internet, it is now possible to work anywhere to work everywhere and so there is little incentive to relocate. Any savings I acquire and not spend on leisure and holidays, I will prefer to spend always looking at what improvements I can make to my existing home.

In terms of my health, I would hope that it will be kept on an even knell with the odd cold during the winter months for as long as possible. I now fully understand that alcohol can no longer play in my life at any time in my future, and I am very committed to that happening. I am also very aware that as I get older, I am likely to be confronted with a range of new and unexpected health related challenges that will further develop my understanding of my body as the management of my health gradually evolves over time. I feel I have a positive attitude that will enable me to embrace my old age with a smile.

In terms of my personal support, I hope it can remain as it is now for as long as possible. I am aware that Flora can not work for me forever as no personal assistant can do that, it is the whole nature of my role as my life moves on. I would also hope the annual supply of live-in volunteers would continue for an indefinite basis because amongst many other things, they help me to stay young in how I feel. I am quite interested to find out at what age if any that the age gap between myself and my volunteers makes the project no longer suitable for my needs? Does the fact I have never conformed well to social norms mean that I may avoid turning into a passive older person? I very much hope so.

In terms of my family and friends, while I may have the occasional vaguely friendly conversations with some of my family members on social media from time to time, I can never imagine ever having a meaningful relationship with any of them in the future. There has been too much water under the bridge and too many old wounds that should simply be left alone as opening them would not help anyone. My relationship with Patrick, my best friend, is as strong as it is ever going to be and I have a good network of friends on social model. I hope to develop more friends via social media and built the relationship further into more 'real world friendships'

In terms of technology, I have always been good at absorbing new technology and making the most of it, bringing it into adapting the way I live, work and play. We will never know what technology will bring us and I have always found that exciting as I am happy to sometimes be a boy with his toys. Technology has liberated me as someone with as a significant impairment more than anything else, and I know it will continue to liberate me in ways I can not currently imagine as the same way it has in the past.

In terms of my work and activism, this is now the area of growth and development that I need to now work on, as everything else now feels in place. I am aware some people say that if you have a certain of level of impairment where there are barriers to paid employment that your contribution to society should be in measured in these terms, and I do agree to some degree, but I also feel far more people with impairments can do paid work, if it is the right kind of work for them, then most other activists would care to admit.

For me, getting paid for the work I am able to do is very important to my self worth and my place in society in terms of having power and influence. This is what makes me happy and what makes me tick. I believe in the power of the individual over the collective and it is a strong viewpoint that I am never likely to change. My employment goal is to be a good amount of money on a regular basis for the work I am capable and best suited into within the timeframes provided to me by my impairment, health and others needs.

I wish to be financially wealthy enough not to have to worry about money in the long term, but it is not just about the money but also, I want what I do and what I achieve to help others in terms of the bigger picture as well as real people in real situations. It is important to be able to assist in the development of relevant and meaningful policy, but it is also important to be able to be involved in really implementing that policy on the ground to make an effective impact for individuals however large or small.

I am determined to focus going forward on obtaining more work, specifically focusing on social care issues as the field currently seems more willing to listen to my ideas then in terms of disability and welfare issues. I believe this is where my golden egg could lie, and I believe it is worthwhile to focus my marketing in this area for at least the next year or so, as well as always being open to any work opportunities that come my way whatever and wherever they may be.

And finally, in terms of my general personhood, I am always going to be a controversial non-conformist in a controversial non-conformist manner. I am privileged to live in a period in history where, as someone with a significant impairment, I have been able to liberate myself enough to most be able to live, work and play in the manner I have chosen, which is tolerated by others even if it was not accepted by others. I also live in a time where I don't have to be accepted by others to be myself. I want to continue to be who I am and who I can be in terms of how I live, how I dress experimenting with different clothing, what I eat experiencing a range of foods, the activities I try, the people I have conversations with, the subjects I find interest in and so on.

Looking back at my story as a whole, I am exceptionally pleased. I have made the most of my life, and I have taken full advantage of many of the opportunities made available to me in the same way they were made available to be peers. I have made many mistakes on many issues and I hope that I have learnt from a lot of them, I believe making mistakes are a part of our learning that enriches our lives, and I am glad I had opportunities to make mistakes as someone considered a responsible person.

I have laughed and cried, been happy and sad, angry and bemused, and all the rainbow of emotions in between. I have had the opportunity to travel locally, nationally and internationally, and to make so many people with so many experiences from so many backgrounds and viewpoints. With the internet, I have been able to have the tools to access so much information so I am able to attempt to have my own educated opinion on a wide range of issues regardless of what anyone. And fundamentally, in the overall balance of everything, I have a happy, enjoyable, rewarding, worthwhile life I would not swap for anything, even when life has its dark moments since they make the light ones brighter.

So at over 52000 words over 35 chapters, this is my story. I am not suggesting for one minute it has been the best story ever written or that my life has been super special, but I believe it is has been interested. I have provided you with the privilege in delving into my deepest parts of my mind and hearing a perspective that may not often been heard before, and I hope you have enjoyed it!

Printed in Great Britain
by Amazon

68846715R00090